WILLIAMS-SONOMA

Cooking for Yourself

GENERAL EDITOR
Chuck Williams

RECIPES
Janet Fletcher

PHOTOGRAPHY
Richard Eskite

TIME
LIFE
BOOKS

TIME-LIFE BOOKS
Time-Life Books is a division of Time Life Inc.
Time-Life is a trademark of Time Warner Inc. U.S.A.

TIME-LIFE CUSTOM PUBLISHING
Vice President and Publisher: Terry Newell
Vice President of Sales and Marketing: Neil Levin
Director of Financial Operations: J. Brian Birky
Director of Acquisitions: Jennifer L. Pearce

WILLIAMS-SONOMA
Founder and Vice-Chairman: Chuck Williams
Book Buyer: Victoria Kalish

WELDON OWEN INC.
President: John Owen
Vice President and Publisher: Wendely Harvey
Chief Operating Officer: Larry Partington
Vice President International Sales: Stuart Laurence
Associate Publisher: Lisa Atwood
Managing Editor: Val Cipollone
Consulting Editor: Norman Kolpas
Copy Editor: Sharon Silva
Design: Kari Perin, Perin+Perin
Production Director: Stephanie Sherman
Production Manager: Jen Dalton
Production Editor: Sarah Lemas
Food Stylist: Pouké
Prop Stylist: Sara Slavin
Prop Assistant: Sarah Dawson
Photo Production Coordinator: Juliann Harvey
Photo Assistant: Kevin Hossler
Food Styling Assistant: Jeff Tucker
Glossary Illustrations: Alice Harth

A NOTE ON WEIGHTS AND MEASURES
All recipes include customary U.S. and metric
measurements. Metric conversions are based on a
standard developed for these books and have been
rounded off. Actual weights may vary.

The Williams-Sonoma Lifestyles Series
conceived and produced by Weldon Owen Inc.
814 Montgomery Street, San Francisco, CA 94133

In collaboration with Williams-Sonoma
3250 Van Ness Avenue, San Francisco, CA 94109

Separations by Colourscan Overseas Co. Pte. Ltd.
Printed in Singapore by Tien Wah Press (Pte.) Ltd.

A WELDON OWEN PRODUCTION
Copyright © 1999 Weldon Owen Inc.
All rights reserved, including the right of
reproduction in whole or in part in any form.

First printed in 1999
10 9 8 7 6 5 4 3 2 1

Library of Congress
Cataloging-in-Publication Data

Fletcher, Janet Kessel.
Cooking for yourself / general editor, Chuck Williams;
  recipes by Janet Fletcher; photography by Richard
  Eskite.
      p. cm. — (Williams-Sonoma lifestyles)
  Includes index.
  ISBN 0-7370-2012-1
  1. Cookery for one. I. Williams, Chuck.
II. Fletcher, Janet Kessel. III. Title IV. Series.
TX652.F56 1999
  641.5′61— dc21   98-35970
                                          CIP

A NOTE ON NUTRITIONAL ANALYSIS
Each recipe is analyzed for significant nutrients per
serving. Not included in the analysis are ingredients
that are optional or added to taste, or are suggested
as an alternative or substitution either in the recipe
or in the recipe introduction or accompanying tip. In
recipes that yield a range of servings, the analysis is
for the middle of that range.

Contents

Welcome

Some of the meals I enjoy the most are those that I cook and eat by myself. Like sitting down with a good book or listening to beautiful music, preparing dinner for one gives me the chance to wind down at the end of a busy day. It's my favorite way of relaxing.

This book is dedicated to the notion that cooking for yourself is not only easy and fun but rewarding—whether you're on your own full-time or part-time. It begins with some ideas to inspire you in preparing and serving your meal, as well as practical information on pantry staples, the equipment you'll need, flavorful bites, and beverages.

Following these introductory pages are 46 recipes expressly developed to yield a single perfect, satisfying serving, sometimes with just a bit left over. Look through them, however, and you'll quickly notice that they make no compromises on quality. Most are simply scaled-down versions of dishes that might ordinarily yield four or six servings.

After all, you deserve well-prepared wonderful food every day, whether you're dining with others or cooking for yourself.

A Table for One

On a sunny afternoon, a tray transports lunch for one, here a flavorful Salade Niçoise (page 20). A wooden table and chair transform the porch into a casual outdoor dining room.

Choosing a Setting

In *The Art of Eating*, M.F.K. Fisher offered "one person dining alone, usually upon a couch or a hillside" as a possible formula for "gastronomical perfection." With her customary clarity and eloquence, the legendary food writer captured the importance of selecting an appropriate setting for enjoying a meal you cook for yourself.

As Fisher's recommendation of a couch might suggest, comfort is paramount. After all, if you're eating on your own, why not pamper yourself? Arrange a place setting at the coffee table in front of the sofa or on a side table next to your favorite armchair. The idea of dining alone on a hillside serves as a reminder that a meal eaten solo can be taken just about wherever you choose to go. If you have a terrace, patio, or garden, and the weather is nice, move your meal outdoors. Your time spent dining alone can be some of the most flexible time you have all day.

By the same token, dining alone affords you the freedom to take your time, relaxing for a few minutes with something to drink and a few savory bites before the meal is ready. It lets you move freely between courses, enabling the simple pleasure of taking dessert and a warm cup of tea by the fireside.

Of course, this is not to say that every meal you cook for yourself needs to be served in a setting considered out of the ordinary. Regular venues such as the kitchen counter, a breakfast nook, or the dining table are all perfectly well suited to the individual diner.

Creating a Mood

The spirit with which you cook has the most to do with creating a comfortable and comforting mood. Preparing food for yourself, morning, noon, or night, is just as important as any other daily activity. It is also, however, a lot of fun. It's private time, which can be hard to come by, and presents an opportunity to indulge the senses and the body, too. Time spent cooking can be relaxing, calming, and uplifting as well. Most important, it's a practical way of doing something good for yourself.

Certainly, the setting you choose and the way you choose to dress it both have a lot to do with mood. You'll find a few simple touches go a long way toward making patio, dining room, or fireside dining really pleasurable.

Flowers are likely candidates, whether placed on the kitchen counter or on the dining table. It takes just a few stems to brighten the room. Candles, too, help set a mood with remarkable ease. A single votive or taper placed nearby casts a peaceful glow.

Music is not only pleasurable to dine by, but can keep you company in the kitchen as well. Once dinner is ready, you may choose to bring a companionable book or magazine to the table. Or, if quiet enjoyment is what you're after, just relax and appreciate the delights of a great meal had in a peaceful setting.

The fireside (above, left) is an inviting spot for finishing the evening meal. Flowers gathered from the garden or bought at a shop (above) are one of the easiest ways to brighten a room, be it the kitchen, dining room, or living area.

Planning Ahead

With all of the wonderful fresh produce available, it's hard to resist leaving the market without more than necessary. Try to buy what you need (above) when you need it. A well-stocked pantry (right) is a cook's best friend.

Stocking Your Pantry

Like cooking in quantity, cooking for yourself becomes easier when you have a selection of staple ingredients at the ready. The following tips, combined with your own personal tastes, will give you a good idea of what to stock in your own kitchen.

Many basic ingredients keep well in the cupboard at cool room temperature, including olive and vegetable oils; vinegars; flavor boosters such as prepared mustards, garlic, dried herbs and spices, salt and whole peppercorns, and extracts (essences) such as vanilla; dried noodles and pastas; dried beans, lentils, and split peas; flour, cereals, and rice; and granulated and brown sugars. Good-quality chocolate and cocoa should also be included. Nuts may be kept on the shelf, too, although once their packages are opened, they are best stored airtight in the freezer.

It also makes sense to keep certain canned goods in your pantry. Two of the most useful items are good-quality, low-sodium broth, particularly chicken broth, and small cans of peeled and chopped tomatoes.

Buying Perishables

There's really no way around buying fresh produce as you need to use it. Some produce does keep well in a cool place. A well-stocked produce bin will likely include onions, bell peppers (capsicums), perhaps a few fresh chiles, a couple of potatoes, and some lemons or limes.

Dairy items are certainly perishable, although some last longer than others. Along with whatever kind of milk you prefer, consider keeping on hand at least half a dozen eggs; a few sticks of butter, which also freeze well; some basic cheeses such as Parmesan, mozzarella, and cheddar; and some yogurt.

When shopping for ultra-perishable items—seafood, poultry, meats—don't hesitate to ask a purveyor to wrap up a small amount. A few sea scallops, a single chicken breast, or one fresh sausage may be all you need for a satisfying meal.

Being Well Equipped

Having equipment of the proper size makes cooking for yourself easy and successful. Single-sized portions cooked in vessels that are too large run the risk of overcooking, drying out, or burning, a circumstance easily prevented by using appropriately sized pots and pans. You'll find plenty of cookware that is perfectly suited to cooking for one.

A small saucepan; an 8-inch (20-cm) sauté pan; a small colander; and individual-sized oven-to-table ware, including baking and gratin dishes of various shapes and round ramekins, are all well worth having on hand.

Flavorful Bites

An assortment of flavorful bites (above) includes bleu d'Auvergne, Camembert, herbed goat cheese, and Gruyère; fresh radishes; crackers and bread; and black and green olives. An assortment of seasonal fruits (below) features apricots, peaches, cherries, and figs—an edible still life that's perfect for eating in between meals or as a simple dessert.

A collection of good recipes makes preparing lunch and dinner no trouble at all. But eating well between these meals can be a challenge. One way to handle the need to have just a little something to calm the appetite is to keep a selection of robust foods on hand. Cheeses, cured meats, oil-cured olives, bite-sized vegetables, fresh fruits, and nuts all fit into this category. Foods such as these can also be used to round out the main course at lunchtime or supper.

Shop for many of these items in a delicatessen or the specialty-foods section of your local market. There you are likely to find a good selection of both black and green olives as well as other pickled or cured vegetables to nibble on with a before-dinner drink or while you're cooking. One particular advantage to such specialties is that most markets will sell them by weight, allowing you to take home quantities as small as you like.

The cheese counter should not be missed. Treat yourself and purchase small amounts of a variety of cheeses you haven't tasted before, then round out your new choices with an old favorite, whether a soft-ripened, blue-veined, or goat cheese. Don't forget to bring home bread, flat bread, or crackers to pair with your selections.

Charcuterie, including cured and prepared meats such as salami and pâté, is another possibility.

Look for other good foods to have on hand in the produce section. Consider, for example, buying a few baby carrots, green (spring) onions, radishes, cherry tomatoes, button mushrooms, or other bite-sized vegetables to make up a plate of crudités. Fresh fruits such as grapes, cherries or other small stone fruits, or a perfect pear or apple make wonderful stand-alone snacks, are fine accompaniments to after-dinner cheeses, or may be served on their own as simple desserts.

Beverages

Food and drink are natural partners, and the beverage you choose for yourself can contribute a great deal to the pleasure you take from a meal.

Many people like to unwind with an aperitif before dining. If your health and lifestyle allow, there's no reason why you shouldn't enjoy alcohol in moderation when you cook for your-

bottles, also called splits. If you open a full-sized bottle with your meal, be sure to replace the cork or seal the bottle with a reusable wine stopper; this will keep out air and prevent the wine from oxidizing so you can enjoy it over the next couple of days. You might also want to seek out special stoppers that remove air from bottles, which will further

self. A glass of dry sherry, a mixture of bitters and soda or freshly squeezed orange juice, a glass of white wine, or your own favorite cocktail are all possibilities.

White or red wine may also accompany the meal itself. In anticipation of times when you might enjoy a glass or two, shop at a well-stocked wine store for half bottles, equivalent to about three glasses, or for quarter

extend a wine's drinkability. With particularly robust dishes, consider a bottle of beer in place of wine.

Of course, alcohol is not a prerequisite to enjoying any meal. Indulge yourself with a favorite beverage of your choosing, whether iced tea or coffee, sparkling water with a wedge of lime, or fresh fruit juice. The options are nearly endless.

Made with minimal effort, drinks plain and fancy elevate a meal. Bitters such as Campari (far left) can be mixed with blood-orange juice or a splash of soda and a twist of orange zest. Half and full bottles of wine and sparkling wine (center) add to the appreciation of well-prepared food. Slices of cucumber and a mint sprig, or wedges of citrus fruit, add fresh color and flavor to sparkling water (above).

Planning Menus

Many of the recipes in this book make excellent single-dish meals, and a number of them incorporate generous side dishes. All of the recipes may also be paired with simply prepared salads, vegetables, grains, or breads, as you like, making a more complete menu for one. The 10 menus shown here represent only a handful of possibilities. You can spend as little or as much time as you like preparing a satisfying meal. Throughout this book you'll find a variety of recipes to suit your needs.

Sunday Dinner

Braised Chicken Provençale
PAGE 58

Sautéed Green Beans

Coarse Country Bread

Lemon Custard
PAGE 96

Provençale Menu

Assorted Cheeses and
Crisp Flat Breads

Braised Tuna with Eggplant,
Tomato, and Olives
PAGE 57

Fresh Figs

Spring Lunch

Iced Tea

Asparagus Frittata with
Prosciutto and Mint
PAGE 42

Ripe Cherries

Bistro Fare

Red Wine

Rosemary Lamb Chops with
Scalloped Potatoes
PAGE 52

Steamed Spinach

Individual Apple Crisp
PAGE 99

Fireside Supper

White Wine

Shaved Mushroom, Fennel,
and Parmesan Salad

Steamed Clams with White
Wine, Garlic, and Parsley
PAGE 71

Coarse Country Bread

Wintertime Favorites

Tossed Green Salad

Spicy Macaroni and Cheese
PAGE 88

Poached Pear with
Ginger Syrup
PAGE 106

Vegetarian Gourmet

Endive and Walnut Salad

Spring Vegetable Stew
with Couscous
PAGE 87

Strawberries with
Crème Fraîche

Summertime Feast

Radishes, Baguette, and Butter

Fettuccine with Cherry
Tomatoes, Arugula, and
Bread Crumbs
PAGE 79

Sliced Peach with Whipped
Ricotta and Honey
PAGE 103

Late-Night Supper

White Wine

Omelet with Spinach
and Blue Cheese
PAGE 38

Baguette

Asian Flavors

Green Mango, Apple, and
Red Onion Salad

Chinese Noodles with
Chicken and Baby Bok Choy
PAGE 94

Fortune Cookies

Warm Spinach Salad with Bacon and Potatoes

PREP TIME: 10 MINUTES

COOKING TIME: 25 MINUTES

INGREDIENTS

¼ lb (125 g) red boiling potatoes
   (1 large or 2 small)

1 egg

salt to taste

¼ lb (125 g) baby spinach leaves,
   tough stems removed

¼ red (Spanish) onion, thinly sliced

2 slices bacon, cut into pieces ½ inch
   (12 mm) wide

1½ teaspoons sherry vinegar or red
   wine vinegar, or to taste

ground pepper to taste

On a night when you prefer to eat lightly, make spinach salad your main course, accompanied by a slice or two of crusty bread or a bakery roll. On another occasion, replace the spinach with young arugula (rocket).

❀ Place the potatoes and egg in a small saucepan with water to cover. Place over medium-high heat, bring to a simmer, and adjust the heat to maintain a gentle simmer. Using a slotted spoon, remove the egg after 8 minutes and run under cold water until cool. Add salt to the water and continue cooking the potatoes until easily pierced with a knife, 5–10 minutes longer. Drain and let cool, then peel if desired. Slice ¼ inch (6 mm) thick (if using a large potato, halve lengthwise first). Peel the hard-boiled egg and quarter it lengthwise.

❀ In a bowl, combine the spinach and red onion. Add the sliced potato.

❀ Put the bacon in a cold frying pan and place over medium heat. Cook until the bacon begins to crisp and has rendered much of its fat, about 5 minutes.

❀ Add the bacon and bacon fat to the spinach mixture and toss well. Add the 1½ teaspoons vinegar, salt, and pepper. Toss again, then taste and adjust the seasonings.

❀ Transfer to a bowl. Arrange the egg wedges around the edge.

NUTRITIONAL ANALYSIS PER SERVING: Calories 455 (Kilojoules 1,911); Protein 15 g; Carbohydrates 28 g; Total Fat 32 g; Saturated Fat 11 g; Cholesterol 243 mg; Sodium 452 mg; Dietary Fiber 5 g

Yellow Split Pea Soup

PREP TIME: 15 MINUTES

COOKING TIME: 1½ HOURS

INGREDIENTS

1 tablespoon vegetable oil

¼ teaspoon cumin seeds

1 large shallot, minced

1 clove garlic, minced

½ cup (3½ oz/105 g) yellow split peas

2 cups (16 fl oz/500 ml) chicken broth

1 small carrot, peeled and diced

2 oz (60 g) green beans, trimmed and cut into ½-inch (12-mm) lengths

1 cup (8 fl oz/250 ml) water

1 tablespoon chopped fresh cilantro (fresh coriander)

salt and ground pepper to taste

A pinch of toasted cumin seeds gives this soup a seductive fragrance. Enjoy any leftovers for lunch the next day; if desired, add a few tablespoons of minced ham when reheating.

MAKES 2 SERVINGS

❋ In a 3-qt (3-l) saucepan over medium-high heat, warm the vegetable oil. When the oil is hot, add the cumin seeds. When the cumin seeds become fragrant and begin to darken, after about 1 minute, add the shallot and garlic. Cook, stirring, until the shallot is softened and beginning to color, about 2 minutes, reducing the heat if necessary to prevent burning.

❋ Stir in the split peas and broth and bring to a simmer. Cover, adjust the heat to maintain a gentle simmer, and cook until the split peas are soft, about 45 minutes. Add the carrot, green beans, and water. Cover and simmer gently, stirring occasionally, until the split peas have dissolved into a near purée, about 30 minutes longer.

❋ Stir in the cilantro, cover, and simmer for 5 minutes to blend the flavors. Season with salt and pepper. Ladle into a warmed bowl.

NUTRITIONAL ANALYSIS PER SERVING: Calories 591 (Kilojoules 2,482); Protein 31 g; Carbohydrates 78 g; Total Fat 19 g; Saturated Fat 3 g; Cholesterol 0 mg; Sodium 2,044 mg; Dietary Fiber 9 g

Salade Niçoise

PREP TIME: 15 MINUTES

COOKING TIME: 30 MINUTES

INGREDIENTS

FOR THE DRESSING
2 teaspoons red wine vinegar

1 teaspoon Dijon mustard

2 anchovy fillets in olive oil, finely
minced

1 small clove garlic, minced

1½ tablespoons olive oil

salt and ground pepper to taste

⅓ lb (155 g) fresh ahi tuna or 1 can
(6 oz/185 g) tuna, preferably oil
packed

3 teaspoons olive oil, if using fresh
tuna

salt and ground pepper to taste

⅓ lb (155 g) small red boiling potatoes

1 egg

1 cup (8 fl oz/250 ml) water

¼ lb (125 g) green and yellow beans,
trimmed

6 butter (Boston) lettuce leaves

1 small tomato, cut into 6 wedges

8 small black olives, preferably
Niçoise

In the south of France in summer, almost every café serves *salade niçoise*, a melange of seasonal vegetables, anchovies, and canned tuna. To improve on a classic, make the salad with baked fresh tuna and add a pungent anchovy-garlic dressing.

❁ To make the dressing, in a small bowl, whisk together the vinegar, mustard, anchovies, and garlic. Slowly whisk in the olive oil. Season with salt and pepper. Set aside to allow the flavors to blend while you prepare the rest of the salad.

❁ If using fresh tuna, preheat an oven to 375°F (190°C). Put the tuna in a baking dish, add 1 teaspoon of the olive oil, and turn to coat with the oil. Season with salt and pepper. Bake until the tuna is opaque throughout and just flakes with a fork, 10–15 minutes. Remove from the oven, let cool, and then flake with your hands into a bowl. Toss with the remaining 2 teaspoons olive oil and set aside. If using canned tuna, drain, break into chunks, and set aside.

❁ Place the potatoes and egg in a small saucepan and add water to cover. Place over medium-high heat, bring to a simmer, and then adjust the heat to maintain a gentle simmer. Using a slotted spoon, remove the egg after 8 minutes and run under cold water until cool. Add salt to the water and continue cooking the potatoes until easily pierced with a knife, 5–10 minutes longer, and then lift them out with the slotted spoon and set aside to cool.

❁ Add the 1 cup (8 fl oz/250 ml) water to the saucepan and some salt. Raise the heat to high and bring the water to a boil. Add the beans and cook until just tender, about 5 minutes. Drain and refresh under cold running water to halt the cooking. Drain well, pat dry, and then cut in half crosswise, if you like.

❁ Peel the hard-boiled egg and quarter it lengthwise. Peel the potatoes and slice ¼ inch (6 mm) thick.

❁ Arrange the lettuce leaves in a large bowl or on a large plate. Top with the tuna, potatoes, egg, beans, and tomato wedges, arranging attractively. Scatter the olives over the salad, and then drizzle with the dressing.

NUTRITIONAL ANALYSIS PER SERVING: Calories 774 (Kilojoules 3,251); Protein 51 g; Carbohydrates 42 g; Total Fat 45 g; Saturated Fat 7 g; Cholesterol 284 mg; Sodium 664 mg; Dietary Fiber 7 g

Eggs with Sweet Peppers, Tomato, and Ham

PREP TIME: 15 MINUTES

COOKING TIME: 25 MINUTES

INGREDIENTS

1 tablespoon olive oil

3 green (spring) onions, white and pale green parts only, minced

1 clove garlic, minced

½ green bell pepper (capsicum), seeded and thinly sliced

½ cup (3 oz/90 g) grated plum (Roma) tomato (see glossary, page 111)

1 small bay leaf

salt and ground pepper to taste

1 teaspoon unsalted butter

1 large, thin slice cooked ham, 2–3 oz (60–90 g)

3 eggs, lightly beaten

Enjoy this French Basque specialty, known as a *pipérade,* with a baguette and a butter (Boston) lettuce salad. You can add the remainder of the bell pepper to your salad, if you like.

❁ In a small frying pan over medium heat, warm the olive oil. Add the green onions and garlic and sauté for about 1 minute to soften them and release their fragrance. Add the bell pepper, cover, and reduce the heat to medium-low. Cook until the pepper is tender, 12–15 minutes.

❁ Add the tomato and bay leaf, season with salt and pepper, and cook uncovered, stirring often, until the mixture is thick, about 5 minutes. Add a little water if the mixture gets too thick. Remove the bay leaf and discard.

❁ While the sauce simmers, in an 8-inch (20-cm) nonstick frying pan over medium heat, melt the butter. Cut the ham into 4 equal pieces, add to the hot frying pan, and sauté, turning once, until lightly browned, about 1 minute on each side. Transfer to a plate and keep warm.

❁ Add the eggs to the tomato sauce and season with salt and pepper. Cook over medium-low heat, stirring constantly and scraping the sides and bottom of the pan with a spatula, until the mixture is thick, about 5 minutes. The eggs will not form large curds but will gradually set into a smooth, creamy, tomatoey mass.

❁ Spoon the eggs into a bowl and put the ham on top.

NUTRITIONAL ANALYSIS PER SERVING: Calories 561 (Kilojoules 2,356); Protein 37 g; Carbohydrates 15 g; Total Fat 39 g; Saturated Fat 11 g; Cholesterol 690 mg; Sodium 1,270 mg; Dietary Fiber 3 g

Potato and Leek Soup with Dill

PREP TIME: 10 MINUTES

COOKING TIME: 30 MINUTES

INGREDIENTS

1 tablespoon unsalted butter

1 small leek, white and pale green parts only, halved and thinly sliced

1 small baking potato, about ½ lb (250 g), halved lengthwise and thinly sliced

salt and ground pepper to taste

1 cup (8 fl oz/250 ml) chicken broth

½ cup (4 fl oz/125 ml) water

¼ cup (2 fl oz/60 ml) heavy (double) cream

1½ teaspoons minced fresh dill

This creamy winter soup departs from the classic French recipe in the last-minute addition of fragrant fresh dill. On another occasion, substitute fresh tarragon for the dill.

❀ In a saucepan over medium-low heat, melt the butter. Add the leek, stir to coat with the butter, cover, and cook, stirring occasionally, until the leek is soft, about 10 minutes. Add the potato and season with salt and pepper. Add the broth and water. Raise the heat to medium-high and bring to a simmer. Cover, adjust the heat to maintain a gentle simmer, and cook until the potatoes are completely tender, about 15 minutes. Remove from the heat and let cool slightly.

❀ In a food processor or blender, purée the soup until completely smooth. Return to the saucepan and stir in the cream and dill. Reheat gently. Taste and adjust the seasonings.

❀ Ladle into a warmed mug or bowl.

NUTRITIONAL ANALYSIS PER SERVING: Calories 535 (Kilojoules 2,247); Protein 9 g; Carbohydrates 47 g; Total Fat 36 g; Saturated Fat 21 g; Cholesterol 113 mg; Sodium 1,050 mg; Dietary Fiber 5 g

Chicken Noodle Soup

PREP TIME: 10 MINUTES

COOKING TIME: 1¼ HOURS IF
USING FRESH NOODLES;
1½ HOURS IF USING DRIED

INGREDIENTS

4 chicken wings, each cut at the joints
into 3 pieces

4 cups (32 fl oz/1 l) water

½ yellow onion stuck with 1 whole
clove

2 fresh parsley sprigs

1 bay leaf

1 small carrot, peeled and diced

1 small celery stalk, diced

salt and ground pepper to taste

2 oz (60 g) dried egg noodles or
fresh fettuccine, broken or cut
into 3-inch (7.5-cm) lengths

COOKING TIP: Instead of pasta, add
¼ cup (2 oz/60 g) rice to the soup
15 minutes before it is done.

On a cold night, hot soup is the ultimate comfort food—especially when it's a nourishing bowl of chicken, vegetables, and egg noodles. Precede it with a salad of escarole (Batavian endive) and apple and follow with a favorite bakery cookie or two.

MAKES 2 SERVINGS

✾ In a 3-qt (3-l) saucepan over medium heat, combine the chicken and water. Bring to a simmer, skimming off any foam that forms on the surface. Add the onion, parsley, and bay leaf, adjust the heat to maintain a gentle simmer, and cook, uncovered, for 20 minutes. Add the carrot and celery and continue to simmer gently, uncovered, until the broth is flavorful, about 40 minutes longer.

✾ Using tongs or a slotted spoon, remove and discard the onion, parsley, and bay leaf. Then transfer the chicken pieces to a cutting board; cut off and discard the wing tips. When cool enough to handle, skin and remove the meat from the remaining pieces. Return the meat to the broth. Season the soup with salt and pepper.

✾ Bring a saucepan three-fourths full of salted water to a boil over high heat. Add the noodles and cook until slightly underdone. The timing will depend upon the noodles used; fresh noodles will take only 1 or 2 minutes, while dried noodles will take up to 10 minutes. Drain and transfer to the soup, then simmer gently for 1 minute.

✾ Ladle into a warmed bowl.

NUTRITIONAL ANALYSIS PER SERVING: Calories 411 (Kilojoules 1,726); Protein 35 g; Carbohydrates 52 g; Total Fat 7 g; Saturated Fat 2 g; Cholesterol 120 mg; Sodium 347 mg; Dietary Fiber 5 g

Baked Goat Cheese Salad with Tomato Bruschetta

PREP TIME: 15 MINUTES

COOKING TIME: 10 MINUTES

INGREDIENTS

1½ tablespoons plus 1 teaspoon
   extra-virgin olive oil

1½ teaspoons red wine vinegar

1 small shallot, minced

salt and ground pepper to taste

3 oz (90 g) fresh goat cheese, patted
   into a round, ½ inch (12 mm) thick

4 slices coarse country bread, each
   about 4 by 2 inches (10 by 5 cm)

1 clove garlic, halved

1 ripe plum (Roma) tomato, halved

3 oz (90 g) mixed baby salad greens
   (about 3 handfuls)

PREP TIP: Mixed baby salad greens sold in bulk may look clean at the market, but they should be washed and dried again at home.

The creamy baked goat cheese popularized in California restaurants makes an easy dinner for one when served with a generous portion of greens and some tomato-rubbed toasts. Buy a young, soft goat cheese that can be shaped, if necessary, into a round between two sheets of waxed paper.

❋ Preheat an oven to 350°F (180°C).

❋ In a small bowl, whisk together the 1½ tablespoons olive oil, vinegar, shallot, salt, and pepper to form a vinaigrette. Set aside.

❋ Put the remaining 1 teaspoon oil in a small baking dish. Add the goat cheese and turn to coat both sides with the oil. Bake until very soft and beginning to lose its shape, about 8 minutes. Keep warm.

❋ Toast the bread slices on both sides in a toaster oven (or slip under a preheated broiler/griller). While hot, rub one side of each bread slice well with the cut garlic clove. Holding the tomato halves cut sides down, rub them vigorously over the garlicky side of each bread slice until each slice is liberally covered with tomato pulp and juice. Drizzle with a little of the vinaigrette.

❋ In a bowl, toss the greens with the remaining vinaigrette. Taste and adjust the seasonings. Arrange on a dinner plate. Using a metal spatula, place the warm goat cheese on top of the greens. Grind a little black pepper over the cheese. Surround with the tomato toasts.

NUTRITIONAL ANALYSIS PER SERVING: Calories 645 (Kilojoules 2,709); Protein 23 g; Carbohydrates 38 g; Total Fat 46 g; Saturated Fat 17 g; Cholesterol 39 mg; Sodium 661 mg; Dietary Fiber 4 g

Mexican Vegetable Soup

PREP TIME: 20 MINUTES

COOKING TIME: 45 MINUTES

INGREDIENTS

1 tablespoon vegetable oil

1 small leek, white and pale green
parts only, halved and thinly sliced

1 small carrot, peeled and diced

½ jalapeño chile, seeded and minced

1 small clove garlic, minced

¼ cup (1½ oz/45 g) grated plum
(Roma) tomato (see glossary,
page 111)

2 cups (16 fl oz/500 ml) chicken
broth

1 cup (8 fl oz/250 ml) water

salt to taste

1 bone-in chicken thigh

1 small zucchini (courgette), diced

1 tablespoon chopped fresh cilantro
(fresh coriander)

¾ cup (4½ oz/140 g) corn kernels

SERVING TIP: Serve with corn
tortillas toasted on both sides in
a frying pan over medium-high heat
or warmed in an aluminum foil
packet in the oven.

Make this soup in summer when corn, tomatoes, and zucchini
are at their best. If you like spice, leave the seeds in the chile.
This recipe yields enough for lunch the next day, too.

MAKES 2 SERVINGS

❁ Heat the vegetable oil in a saucepan over medium heat. Add the leek,
carrot, chile, and garlic and sauté until the vegetables are softened, about
5 minutes. Add the tomato and sauté until the flavor develops, about
3 minutes. Add the broth and water. Bring to a simmer and season with
salt. Add the chicken, cover partially, and simmer gently until the chicken
is cooked through, about 20 minutes.

❁ Using tongs, transfer the chicken to a cutting board and let cool. Add
the zucchini and cilantro to the soup and simmer gently until the zucchini is just tender, 5–10 minutes. Stir in the corn and simmer until
tender, about 2 minutes.

❁ Remove and discard the skin from the chicken thigh and then remove
the meat from the bone. Shred or coarsely chop the meat, stir into the
soup, and heat through. Taste and adjust the seasonings.

❁ Ladle into a warmed bowl.

NUTRITIONAL ANALYSIS PER SERVING: Calories 451 (Kilojoules 1,894); Protein 25 g;
Carbohydrates 44 g; Total Fat 22 g; Saturated Fat 4 g; Cholesterol 57 mg; Sodium 2,114 mg;
Dietary Fiber 7 g

Salmon Salad with Beets and Yogurt-Cucumber Dressing

PREP TIME: 20 MINUTES

COOKING TIME: 1¼ HOURS

INGREDIENTS

2 small red, golden, or Chioggia beets

¼ cup (2 fl oz/60 ml) water

1 teaspoon olive oil

1 skinless salmon fillet, 6 oz (185 g)

salt and ground pepper to taste

2 tablespoons dry white wine

FOR THE DRESSING

¼ cup (2 oz/60 g) plain yogurt

1 teaspoon olive oil

1 small clove garlic, minced

1 tablespoon minced fresh dill

1 tablespoon minced green (spring) onion, white and pale green parts only

⅓ cup (1½ oz/45 g) peeled, seeded, and grated cucumber

salt and ground pepper to taste

about 6 pale inner butter (Boston) lettuce leaves

1 lemon wedge

MAKE-AHEAD TIP: While you're taking the time to roast the beets, roast a few extra to add to salads throughout the week.

Consider making this warm salmon salad for a midday meal as well as for dinner. You can also expand it with a few blanched green beans, steamed potatoes, or sliced tomatoes.

❄ Preheat an oven to 400°F (200°C).

❄ Trim off the beet greens, leaving ½ inch (12 mm) of the stem intact, and reserve for another use. Rinse the beets thoroughly, but do not peel. Place in a small baking dish and add the water. Cover tightly and bake until tender when pierced, 45–55 minutes. Remove from the oven, let cool, and then slip off the skins with your fingers or a small knife. Cut in half, then slice thinly or cut into thin wedges. Set aside.

❄ Reduce the oven temperature to 350°F (180°C). Put the olive oil in a small baking dish, add the salmon, and turn to coat with the oil. Season with salt and pepper. Spoon the wine around the fish. Bake until the salmon is opaque throughout and just flakes with a fork, about 15 minutes.

❄ Meanwhile, make the dressing: In a small bowl, whisk together the yogurt, olive oil, garlic, dill, and green onion. Stir in the cucumber. Season with salt and pepper.

❄ Line a dinner plate with the lettuce leaves. Remove the salmon fillet from the oven and place in the center of the plate. Scatter the beet slices over the lettuce. Spoon a little of the dressing over the salmon. Garnish the salad with a lemon wedge and set out the remaining dressing alongside.

NUTRITIONAL ANALYSIS PER SERVING: Calories 527 (Kilojoules 2,213); Protein 39 g; Carbohydrates 23 g; Total Fat 30 g; Saturated Fat 6 g; Cholesterol 108 mg; Sodium 231 mg; Dietary Fiber 2 g

Chopped Chicken Salad with Lemon-Tarragon Dressing

PREP TIME: 25 MINUTES

COOKING TIME: 15 MINUTES

INGREDIENTS

1 skinless, boneless chicken breast half, about ⅓ lb (155 g)

1½ cups (12 fl oz/375 ml) chicken broth, or as needed

FOR THE DRESSING

1½ tablespoons lemon juice, plus more to taste

2 teaspoons minced fresh tarragon

1 teaspoon Dijon mustard

1 small clove garlic, minced

2½ tablespoons olive oil

salt and ground pepper to taste

¼ lb (125 g) romaine (cos) lettuce heart, chopped

¼ small fennel bulb, trimmed and chopped

6 small fresh mushrooms, brushed clean and chopped

5 radishes, chopped

1 small carrot, peeled and chopped

¼ small head radicchio, chopped

¼ small red (Spanish) onion, chopped

COOKING TIP: Use the leftover chicken broth from this recipe for a soup the following day, adding orzo pasta, rice, egg noodles, or store-bought tortellini.

This versatile salad can accommodate the odds and ends of raw vegetables that tend to accumulate in the refrigerator bin. Instead of fennel, mushrooms, or radishes, try cucumber, zucchini (courgette), celery, or cauliflower. Or eliminate the chicken to make a vegetarian version.

❈ In a small saucepan over medium heat, combine the chicken breast half and the 1½ cups (12 fl oz/375 ml) broth, or as needed to cover. Bring to a simmer, adjust the heat to keep the broth just below a simmer, and cook, uncovered, until the chicken is just cooked through, about 10 minutes. Using a slotted spoon, transfer the chicken breast to a cutting board; reserve the broth for another use. When the chicken is cool, cut into small, neat dice.

❈ To make the dressing, in a small bowl, whisk together the 1½ tablespoons lemon juice, tarragon, mustard, and garlic. Gradually whisk in the olive oil. Season with salt and pepper. Set aside to allow the flavors to blend.

❈ In a large bowl, combine the romaine, fennel, mushrooms, radishes, carrot, radicchio, and red onion.

❈ Add the chicken to the dressing and stir to coat, then add the chicken and all the dressing to the vegetables. Toss well. Taste and adjust the seasonings. The salad will probably need more lemon, as it should taste quite lemony.

NUTRITIONAL ANALYSIS PER SERVING: Calories 609 (Kilojoules 2,558); Protein 43 g; Carbohydrates 21 g; Total Fat 39 g; Saturated Fat 6 g; Cholesterol 87 mg; Sodium 1,848 mg; Dietary Fiber 6 g

Shrimp and Corn Chowder

PREP TIME: 20 MINUTES

COOKING TIME: 30 MINUTES

INGREDIENTS

¼ lb (125 g) large shrimp (prawns) in the shell

1½ cups (12 fl oz/375 ml) water

1 slice bacon, diced

3 teaspoons unsalted butter

2 tablespoons minced green (spring) onion, white and pale green parts only

2 teaspoons all-purpose (plain) flour

¼ lb (125 g) boiling potatoes, peeled and diced

¾ cup (4½ oz/140 g) corn kernels

1 cup (8 fl oz/250 ml) milk

1 teaspoon minced fresh parsley

salt and ground pepper to taste

This recipe makes a generous dinner for one. Or you can save some of the chowder for lunch the following day, using only ½ teaspoon butter with each serving. On another occasion, substitute a roasted, peeled, and diced red bell pepper (capsicum) for the corn.

MAKES 2 SERVINGS

❋ Peel the shrimp, then cut each shrimp in half lengthwise, discarding the dark veinlike intestinal tract that runs along its back. Put the shells in a small saucepan with the water. Bring to a simmer over medium heat, adjust the heat to maintain a gentle simmer, and cook for 10 minutes. Strain, discarding the shells. Set the liquid aside.

❋ In a saucepan over medium-low heat, fry the bacon until crisp, about 5 minutes. Using a slotted spoon, transfer to paper towels to drain. Add 2 teaspoons of the butter and the green onion to the saucepan and sauté until the onion is softened, about 1 minute. Stir in the flour and cook, stirring, until smooth and slightly thickened, about 1 minute. Add the potatoes and the strained shrimp broth and bring to a simmer, stirring constantly. Cover and simmer gently until the potatoes are tender, about 10 minutes.

❋ Add the corn, milk, parsley, the reserved shrimp, salt, and pepper to the saucepan and stir well. Bring just to a simmer and stir in the bacon.

❋ Ladle into a warmed bowl and top with the remaining 1 teaspoon butter.

NUTRITIONAL ANALYSIS PER SERVING: Calories 674 (Kilojoules 2,831); Protein 35 g; Carbohydrates 57 g; Total Fat 36 g; Saturated Fat 18 g; Cholesterol 218 mg; Sodium 438 mg; Dietary Fiber 6 g

Omelet with Spinach and Blue Cheese

PREP TIME: 10 MINUTES

COOKING TIME: 10 MINUTES

INGREDIENTS

¼ lb (125 g) spinach leaves, thick
   stems removed

1 teaspoon olive oil

1 small clove garlic, minced

salt and ground pepper to taste

3 eggs

2 teaspoons unsalted butter

1 oz (30 g) mild blue cheese, such
   as Cambozola or Stilton, or fresh
   goat cheese, in small pieces,
   at room temperature

Choose a mild blue cheese or goat cheese for this recipe. A strong blue such as Roquefort, Maytag, or Gorgonzola would overwhelm the delicate eggs.

❀ Rinse and drain the spinach, then put into an 8- to 10-inch (20- to 25-cm) nonstick frying pan or omelet pan with just the rinsing water clinging to the leaves. Cover and cook over medium heat until the spinach wilts, about 3 minutes. Transfer to a sieve and press on the spinach with the back of a wooden spoon to squeeze out the excess moisture. Chop coarsely.

❀ Rinse and dry the frying pan. Return it to medium heat and add the olive oil. When the oil is hot, add the garlic and sauté for 1 minute to release its fragrance. Add the spinach, season lightly with salt and pepper, and cook until just hot throughout. Transfer to a plate.

❀ In a bowl, season the eggs with salt and pepper and whisk to blend. Return the frying pan to medium-high heat and add 1 teaspoon of the butter. When the butter melts, add the eggs. Using the back of a fork or a heat-resistant rubber spatula for a nonstick frying pan, stir the eggs briskly until they begin to set. Allow them to set on the bottom without stirring further, then lift the edges of the omelet with the fork or spatula to allow the uncooked egg to flow underneath.

❀ When the surface is cooked but still moist, put the spinach and the cheese on the two-thirds of the omelet farthest from the pan handle. Using the fork or spatula, fold the closest third of the omelet over onto the middle third. With a warmed dinner plate in one hand and the pan in the other, slide the outer third of the omelet onto the plate, then tilt the pan to flip the rest of the omelet over.

❀ Gloss the surface of the omelet with the remaining 1 teaspoon butter and eat hot.

NUTRITIONAL ANALYSIS PER SERVING: Calories 452 (Kilojoules 1,898); Protein 27 g; Carbohydrates 6 g; Total Fat 36 g; Saturated Fat 15 g; Cholesterol 679 mg; Sodium 650 mg; Dietary Fiber 2 g

Quesadilla with Cheese and Chile

PREP TIME: 10 MINUTES

COOKING TIME: 25 MINUTES

INGREDIENTS

1 Anaheim or poblano chile

1½ teaspoons vegetable oil

2 flour tortillas, each 8 inches
(20 cm) in diameter

2 oz (60 g) Monterey jack cheese,
shredded

salt to taste

¼ cup (¼ oz/7 g) fresh cilantro (fresh
coriander) leaves

1 green (spring) onion, white and
pale green parts only, minced

COOKING TIP: Instead of plain flour
tortillas, you can use vegetable-flavored
ones such as spinach or tomato,
which may be found in well-stocked
food stores.

Mexico's version of a grilled cheese sandwich makes a satisfying supper with a salad of romaine (cos) lettuce, avocado, and radishes. If you like tomato salsa, spoon some over the quesadilla.

✳ Preheat a broiler (griller). Place the chile on a baking sheet, slip under the broiler, and broil (grill), turning as necessary, until the skin blackens and blisters on all sides. Transfer to a cutting board, drape loosely with aluminum foil, and let cool for 10 minutes. Peel away the skin, then remove the stem and seeds. Cut the chile into small dice.

✳ Heat a large frying pan over medium-high heat. Add the oil and swirl to coat the bottom of the pan. When the oil is very hot but not smoking, add 1 of the flour tortillas. Immediately top with the cheese, spreading it evenly. Season with salt, then scatter the chile, cilantro, and green onion evenly over the cheese.

✳ When the cheese is mostly melted and the tortilla is nicely browned on the bottom, after 1–2 minutes, place the remaining tortilla on top. Place one hand, palm down, on the top tortilla to steady the quesadilla. Then, using a long spatula, carefully and quickly turn the quesadilla over in the frying pan. Reduce the heat to medium. Cook on the second side until the bottom is nicely browned, 1–2 minutes longer.

✳ Transfer to a cutting board and cut into wedges. Eat the quesadilla piping hot.

NUTRITIONAL ANALYSIS PER SERVING: Calories 517 (Kilojoules 2,171); Protein 21 g; Carbohydrates 43 g; Total Fat 29 g; Saturated Fat 12 g; Cholesterol 60 mg; Sodium 645 mg; Dietary Fiber 3 g

Asparagus Frittata with Prosciutto and Mint

PREP TIME: 10 MINUTES

COOKING TIME: 25 MINUTES

INGREDIENTS

6 thick asparagus spears

1½ teaspoons unsalted butter

salt and ground pepper to taste

3 eggs

1 large or 2 small thin slices
    prosciutto (½ oz/15 g), minced

2 teaspoons chopped fresh mint

COOKING TIP: A frittata can accommodate almost any vegetable. Substitute sliced mushrooms, onions, or bell peppers for the asparagus, if you like.

The flat Italian-style omelet known as a frittata also makes an excellent sandwich filling. Cut it to fit your choice of bread and, if you like, add greens, tomato, and mayonnaise.

❀ Position a rack in a broiler (griller) 8–10 inches (20–25 cm) from the heat source. Preheat the broiler.

❀ Holding an asparagus spear near the stem end, bend it gently. It will break naturally at the point at which the spear becomes tough. Repeat with the remaining spears, discarding the tough ends. Slice the tender parts on the diagonal into pieces ¼ inch (6 mm) thick, leaving the tips whole.

❀ In a flameproof 8-inch (20-cm) nonstick frying pan over medium heat, melt the butter. Add the asparagus, season with salt and pepper, and sauté until just tender, about 8 minutes, reducing the heat if necessary to prevent browning.

❀ Meanwhile, in a bowl, whisk together the eggs, prosciutto, mint, and several grinds of pepper. When the asparagus are just tender, add the egg mixture to the frying pan and immediately reduce the heat to low. Stir gently with a spatula just to distribute the asparagus evenly, then stop stirring and let the frittata set slowly over low heat, about 15 minutes. It will still be runny on top.

❀ Slip the frying pan under the broiler and broil (grill) briefly to set the top, less than 1 minute. Remove from the broiler and invert a serving dish over the frying pan. Carefully invert the plate and pan together and lift off the pan. Let cool briefly.

❀ Eat the frittata warm, not hot.

NUTRITIONAL ANALYSIS PER SERVING: Calories 327 (Kilojoules 1,373); Protein 26 g; Carbohydrates 5 g; Total Fat 23 g; Saturated Fat 9 g; Cholesterol 665 mg; Sodium 455 mg; Dietary Fiber 1 g

Broiled Cornish Hen al Diavolo

PREP TIME: 15 MINUTES, PLUS
1 HOUR FOR MARINATING

COOKING TIME: 20 MINUTES

INGREDIENTS

1 Cornish hen or poussin, 1¼–1½ lb
(625–750 g)

1½ tablespoons extra-virgin olive oil

1 teaspoon coarsely ground pepper

salt to taste

2 oz (60 g) mixed baby salad greens
(about 2 handfuls)

1 small ripe tomato, cut into wedges,
plus a few yellow pear tomatoes,
halved, if you like

1 lemon wedge

PREP TIP: To grind the pepper
coarsely, use a mortar and pestle,
a spice grinder, or a pepper mill
that may be adjusted to give a
coarse grind.

The liberal use of black pepper explains why Italians call this preparation "devil's style." Arranged on a bed of baby salad greens, the warm chicken releases well-seasoned juices that serve as a salad dressing.

❊ Rinse the bird inside and out. Place breast side up on a cutting board and, using a heavy knife positioned inside the bird, cut down both sides of the backbone to separate it from the body. Discard the backbone or save it for making stock. Turn the bird skin side down and crack the breastbone with the knife so that the bird lies flat. Pat dry with paper towels.

❊ Coat the bird evenly on both sides with the olive oil, pepper, and salt. Place on a platter, cover, and refrigerate for 1 hour; bring to room temperature before cooking.

❊ Position a rack about 8 inches (20 cm) from the broiler (griller) element, then set a broiler pan on the rack. Preheat the broiler for 5 minutes.

❊ Set the bird on the broiler pan, skin side down. Brush with any seasoned oil remaining on the platter. Slip under the broiler and broil (grill) until the juices sizzle and the skin on the legs begins to brown, about 12 minutes. Remove from the broiler and collect any drippings in the bottom of the pan. Turn the bird skin side up, baste with the pan drippings, and return to the broiler. Broil until the skin browns and blisters and the juices run clear when the thickest part of the thigh is pierced, about 8 minutes. Remove from the broiler.

❊ Put the greens on a dinner plate. Top with the bird and arrange the tomato wedges alongside. Drizzle the greens and tomato with 1 tablespoon of drippings from the broiler pan. Garnish the plate with the lemon wedge and be sure to squeeze the lemon over the bird and greens before eating.

NUTRITIONAL ANALYSIS PER SERVING: Calories 909 (Kilojoules 3,818); Protein 61 g; Carbohydrates 12 g; Total Fat 70 g; Saturated Fat 16 g; Cholesterol 345 mg; Sodium 186 mg; Dietary Fiber 3 g

Foil-Baked Salmon with Corn and Lime

PREP TIME: 20 MINUTES

COOKING TIME: 20 MINUTES

INGREDIENTS

¾ cup (4½ oz/140 g) corn kernels

¼ red bell pepper (capsicum), seeded and cut into small, neat dice

2 tablespoons chopped fresh cilantro (fresh coriander)

½ jalapeño chile, seeded and minced, or more to taste

salt and ground pepper to taste

2 teaspoons unsalted butter, cut into bits

1 lime wedge, plus 3 thin lime slices

1 skinless salmon fillet, ½ lb (250 g)

Baking fish and vegetables in a foil packet makes after-dinner cleanup easy. Just transfer the contents to your dinner plate and discard the foil. On another occasion, substitute halibut or shrimp (peeled or not) for the salmon. Add a green salad, if you like.

❀ Preheat an oven to 450°F (230°C).

❀ Put the corn kernels in a bowl. Add the bell pepper, cilantro, chile, salt, and pepper and mix well.

❀ Put a 12-by-18-inch (30-by-45-cm) sheet of heavy-duty aluminum foil on a work surface. Top with the corn mixture and dot with 1 teaspoon of the butter. Squeeze the lime wedge over the salmon fillet, then season with salt and pepper. Place the salmon on top of the corn mixture. Top with lime slices and dot with the remaining 1 teaspoon butter.

❀ Bring the long edges of the foil together and fold over to form a tight seal. Fold and seal the ends as well. Bake until the salmon is opaque throughout and just flakes with a fork, 15–20 minutes. The timing will depend upon the thickness of the fillet.

❀ Transfer the packet to a heatproof work surface. Open the foil carefully at the ends first, allowing hot steam to escape, then unwrap the top. Transfer to a warmed dinner plate.

NUTRITIONAL ANALYSIS PER SERVING: Calories 613 (Kilojoules 2,575); Protein 50 g; Carbohydrates 30 g; Total Fat 34 g; Saturated Fat 10 g; Cholesterol 155 mg; Sodium 157 mg; Dietary Fiber 5 g

Osso Buco

PREP TIME: 25 MINUTES

COOKING TIME: 2½ HOURS

INGREDIENTS

1 tablespoon unsalted butter

1 small leek, white and pale green
   parts only, chopped

1 small carrot, peeled and chopped

1 small celery stalk, chopped

1 clove garlic, minced

½ teaspoon minced fresh marjoram

2 teaspoons minced fresh parsley

1 tablespoon olive oil

1 slice veal shank, about 2 inches
   (5 cm) thick

salt and ground pepper to taste

1 tablespoon all-purpose (plain) flour

⅓ cup (3 fl oz/80 ml) dry white wine

¼ cup (1½ oz/45 g) grated plum
   (Roma) tomato (see glossary,
   page 111) or finely chopped
   canned tomato

¼ cup (2 fl oz/60 ml) chicken broth

COOKING TIP: For best results, don't
try to make this dish ahead. Veal
tends to dry out when reheated.

This classic Milanese dish, which combines a braised veal shank
with aromatic vegetables, can be in the oven in half an hour, but
it does require about 2 hours to bake. While the house fills with
an inviting aroma and the oven does the work, you can relax
with something to read and a glass of wine. At the butcher shop,
ask for a round about 2 inches (5 cm) thick cut from the large
end of the shank, or use two smaller rounds.

❈ Preheat an oven to 325°F (165°C).

❈ In a small ovenproof frying pan over medium-low heat, melt the
butter. Add the leek, carrot, celery, garlic, marjoram, and 1 teaspoon of
the parsley and sauté until the vegetables are tender, about 10 minutes.
Transfer the vegetables to a plate, using a rubber spatula to remove all
the traces from the frying pan.

❈ Return the pan to medium-high heat and add the olive oil. Season
the veal shank with salt and pepper and coat lightly with the flour, shaking off the excess. Place in the pan and turn to brown on all sides,
5–8 minutes total. Transfer the shank to the plate with the vegetables.
Pour off any fat in the pan. Add the white wine to the pan, bring to
a simmer, and deglaze the pan, stirring with a wooden spoon to scrape
up any browned bits on the pan bottom. Continue to simmer until the
wine almost completely evaporates. Return the vegetables and shank to
the frying pan. Add the tomato and broth.

❈ Cover and bake until the veal is fork-tender, about 2 hours. Taste the
sauce and adjust the seasonings.

❈ Transfer the shank to a warmed dinner plate and spoon the sauce
over and around it. Top with the remaining 1 teaspoon parsley.

NUTRITIONAL ANALYSIS PER SERVING: Calories 476 (Kilojoules 1,999); Protein 40 g;
Carbohydrates 23 g; Total Fat 25 g; Saturated Fat 10 g; Cholesterol 167 mg; Sodium 425 mg;
Dietary Fiber 4 g

Pan-Roasted Halibut with Braised Red Onion

PREP TIME: 10 MINUTES

COOKING TIME: 35 MINUTES

INGREDIENTS

2 teaspoons unsalted butter

1 small red (Spanish) onion, halved and thinly sliced

1 teaspoon lemon juice

½ teaspoon minced fresh thyme

salt and ground pepper to taste

1 skinless halibut fillet, 6 oz (185 g)

1 teaspoon olive oil

COOKING TIP: Instead of baking the halibut on the bed of braised onions, toss the onions with fresh fettuccine. They make a delicious, simple sauce.

The lemon juice helps the onion keep its color during the slow cooking that softens and sweetens it. Serve with steamed red potatoes and a green salad.

❈ Preheat an oven to 375°F (190°C).

❈ In an ovenproof frying pan over medium-low heat, melt the butter. Add the onion, lemon juice, thyme, salt, and pepper. Toss to coat the onion with the seasonings, then sauté until soft, about 5 minutes. Cover and cook, stirring occasionally and reducing the heat as necessary to keep the onion from burning, until the onion is soft and sweet, about 15 minutes.

❈ Season the halibut with salt and pepper and place in the frying pan on top of the onion. Bake until the fish is opaque throughout and just flakes with a fork, about 12 minutes. Check once or twice; if the onion appears to be drying out, add a teaspoon or two of water.

❈ Using a spatula, transfer the fish to a warmed dinner plate and drizzle with the olive oil. Put the onion alongside.

NUTRITIONAL ANALYSIS PER SERVING: Calories 342 (Kilojoules 1,436); Protein 37 g; Carbohydrates 11 g; Total Fat 16 g; Saturated Fat 6 g; Cholesterol 75 mg; Sodium 106 mg; Dietary Fiber 2 g

Rosemary Lamb Chops with Scalloped Potatoes

PREP TIME: 15 MINUTES, PLUS
1 HOUR FOR MARINATING

COOKING TIME: 1 HOUR

INGREDIENTS

FOR THE LAMB CHOPS

2 loin lamb chops, about ¼ lb
   (125 g) each

1 tablespoon olive oil

½ teaspoon minced fresh rosemary

1 garlic clove, thinly sliced

ground pepper and salt to taste

FOR THE SCALLOPED POTATOES

1 garlic clove, halved

1 russet potato, about ½ lb (250 g),
   peeled and sliced ⅛ inch (3 mm)
   thick

2 tablespoons minced green (spring)
   onion, white and pale green parts
   only

¼ teaspoon salt

ground pepper to taste

½ cup (4 fl oz/125 ml) heavy (double)
   cream

Treat yourself to a restaurant-quality meal of herbed lamb chops and creamy scalloped potatoes. If you like, cook the chops on a charcoal grill instead of broiling them, or substitute a baked potato to simplify.

❀ To prepare the lamb chops, place them in a shallow dish. Add the olive oil, rosemary, garlic, and pepper. Turn the chops to coat with the seasonings. Let stand at room temperature for 1 hour.

❀ Meanwhile, prepare the potatoes: Preheat an oven to 325°F (165°C). Rub a 9-by-6-inch (23-by-15-cm) oval gratin dish with the cut sides of the garlic clove. Arrange the potato slices in the dish in layers, slightly overlapping the slices and sprinkling the green onion, salt, and pepper between the layers.

❀ In a small saucepan over medium heat, bring the cream to a simmer. Pour the cream over the potatoes, then cover the gratin dish with aluminum foil.

❀ Bake for 30 minutes, then uncover and continue to bake until the potatoes are tender and the cream is absorbed, 10–15 minutes longer. Let rest for 10 minutes before eating.

❀ While the potatoes rest, position a rack in the broiler (griller) about 7 inches (18 cm) from the heat source and preheat the broiler. Transfer the lamb chops to a broiler pan, leaving the garlic behind. Season with salt. Broil for 4 minutes, then turn, season with salt, and broil on the second side until done to your liking, about 3 minutes for medium-rare.

❀ Transfer the lamb chops to a warmed dinner plate. Slide the potatoes from the gratin dish alongside.

NUTRITIONAL ANALYSIS PER SERVING: Calories 853 (Kilojoules 3,583); Protein 22 g; Carbohydrates 42 g; Total Fat 67 g; Saturated Fat 34 g; Cholesterol 222 mg; Sodium 681 mg; Dietary Fiber 4 g

Greek-Style Shrimp with Tomato and Feta

PREP TIME: 20 MINUTES

COOKING TIME: 25 MINUTES

INGREDIENTS

3 teaspoons olive oil

1 clove garlic, minced

2 green (spring) onions, white and pale green parts only

pinch of red pepper flakes

⅔ cup (4 oz/125 g) grated plum (Roma) tomato (see glossary, page 111)

2 teaspoons minced fresh parsley

¼ teaspoon crushed fennel seeds

1 tablespoon dry white wine

salt to taste

⅓ cup (1 oz/30 g) frozen petite peas

6 large shrimp (prawns), about ⅓ lb (155 g), peeled, with last shell segment intact, and deveined

1½ oz (45 g) Greek, French, or Bulgarian feta cheese

PREP TIP: Crush whole fennel seeds in a mortar with a pestle, or use a spice grinder.

A pinch of crushed fennel seeds adds an aromatic note to this popular Greek dish. Before you begin cooking the shrimp, start steaming some rice. Then, while the shrimp bakes and the rice cooks, dress a romaine (cos) salad, and open a bottle of Sauvignon Blanc.

❀ Preheat an oven to 375°F (190°C).

❀ In a frying pan over medium heat, warm 2 teaspoons of the olive oil. Add the garlic, green onions, and red pepper flakes and sauté for 1 minute to release their fragrance. Add the tomato, 1 teaspoon of the parsley, the fennel seeds, wine, and salt. Simmer until thick and tasty, about 5 minutes.

❀ Stir in the peas. Transfer the sauce to a baking dish just large enough to hold the shrimp in a single layer. Top with the shrimp and then with the feta, broken into small clumps. Cover with aluminum foil. Bake until the shrimp are just opaque throughout, about 15 minutes.

❀ Uncover the baking dish and drizzle with the remaining 1 teaspoon olive oil. Garnish with the remaining 1 teaspoon parsley.

NUTRITIONAL ANALYSIS PER SERVING: Calories 431 (Kilojoules 1,810); Protein 34 g; Carbohydrates 15 g; Total Fat 25 g; Saturated Fat 9 g; Cholesterol 224 mg; Sodium 709 mg; Dietary Fiber 4 g

Braised Tuna with Eggplant, Tomato, and Olives

PREP TIME: 15 MINUTES

COOKING TIME: 15 MINUTES

INGREDIENTS

3 teaspoons olive oil

1 Asian (slender) eggplant (aubergine), about 3 oz (90 g), unpeeled, cut into ½-inch (12-mm) dice

salt to taste

1 small clove garlic, minced

⅔ cup (4 oz/125 g) grated plum (Roma) tomato (see glossary, page 111)

4 fresh basil leaves, torn into small pieces

8 Niçoise olives, pitted and coarsely chopped

1 tuna fillet, about 6 oz (185 g), no more than ½ inch (12 mm) thick

ground pepper to taste

The key to preparing fresh tuna, which is very lean, is not to overcook it. Remove from the heat while it is still pink at the center.

❀ In a frying pan over medium-high heat, warm 2 teaspoons of the olive oil. Add the eggplant, season with salt, and sauté until lightly browned, about 3 minutes. Remove from the heat, add the garlic, and stir for about 15 seconds. Return to the heat and add the tomato, basil, and olives. Bring to a simmer, cover, and adjust the heat to maintain a gentle simmer. Cook until the eggplant is just tender, about 5 minutes, adding a little water if the mixture gets too thick.

❀ Season the tuna with salt and pepper, add to the frying pan, and drizzle with the remaining 1 teaspoon olive oil. Cover and simmer gently for 2 minutes, then turn the tuna over, cover, and cook until it just flakes with a fork, about 1½ minutes longer. It should still be pink in the center; do not overcook it or it will be dry.

❀ Using a spatula, transfer the tuna to a warmed dinner plate. If the sauce is a little thin, continue to cook over medium-high heat until reduced to the desired consistency. Spoon the sauce over and around the tuna.

NUTRITIONAL ANALYSIS PER SERVING: Calories 382 (Kilojoules 1,604); Protein 42 g; Carbohydrates 12 g; Total Fat 18 g; Saturated Fat 3 g; Cholesterol 77 mg; Sodium 180 mg; Dietary Fiber 4 g

Braised Chicken Provençale

PREP TIME: 15 MINUTES

COOKING TIME: 30 MINUTES

INGREDIENTS

1 teaspoon olive oil

1 chicken thigh

salt and ground pepper to taste

1 clove garlic, minced

½ cup (3 oz/90 g) grated plum (Roma) tomato (see *glossary*, *page 111*)

1 anchovy fillet in olive oil, minced

1 tablespoon dry white wine

¼ teaspoon minced fresh thyme

8 Niçoise olives, pitted and coarsely chopped

PREP TIP: Some well-stocked food stores carry pitted Niçoise olives. To pit olives easily, smash them gently with the flat side of a chef's knife and then squeeze out the pit.

A chicken thigh is better for braising than a lean chicken breast. It doesn't dry out as quickly, and its fuller flavor can stand up to this zesty sauce.

❀ In a small frying pan over medium-high heat, warm the olive oil. When the oil is hot, add the chicken thigh, skin side down. Season with salt and pepper. Reduce the heat to medium and cook until the skin side is nicely browned, about 3 minutes. Turn, season with salt and pepper, and cook on the second side until nicely browned, about 2 minutes. Transfer the chicken to a small plate.

❀ Remove the frying pan from the heat for 1 minute to cool slightly, then add the garlic. Return to medium-low heat and sauté for about 1 minute to release its fragrance. Add the tomato, anchovy, wine, and thyme. Stir to blend, then return the chicken to the frying pan, skin side up. Cover, adjust the heat to maintain a gentle simmer, and cook, turning the chicken halfway through, until no longer pink at the bone, about 20 minutes.

❀ Using a slotted spoon, transfer the chicken to a warmed dinner plate. Add the olives to the frying pan and cook until heated through. If the sauce is a little thin, continue to cook over medium-high heat until reduced to the desired consistency. Pour the sauce over the chicken.

NUTRITIONAL ANALYSIS PER SERVING: Calories 298 (Kilojoules 1,252); Protein 19 g; Carbohydrates 6 g; Total Fat 22 g; Saturated Fat 5 g; Cholesterol 81 mg; Sodium 330 mg; Dietary Fiber 2 g

Baked Chicken with Mustard, Tarragon, Carrot, and Leek

PREP TIME: 15 MINUTES

COOKING TIME: 40 MINUTES

INGREDIENTS

2 tablespoons chicken broth

2 tablespoons heavy (double) cream

1 teaspoon Dijon mustard

½ teaspoon minced fresh tarragon

salt and ground pepper to taste

1 small leek, white and pale green parts only, halved lengthwise and very thinly sliced

1 small carrot, peeled and very thinly sliced

1 skinless, boneless chicken breast half

SERVING TIP: For an even more substantial main dish, serve the chicken, vegetables, and sauce over a bed of steamed rice or boiled egg noodles.

This dish represents the best of French home cooking. It highlights the harmony between chicken and tarragon, but other herbs would work as well. Try replacing the Dijon mustard and tarragon with honey mustard or a mustard flavored with other minced herbs.

❀ Preheat an oven to 375°F (190°C).

❀ In a bowl, whisk together the chicken broth, cream, mustard, tarragon, salt, and pepper until blended. Mix together the leek and carrot and spread out on the bottom of a baking dish; a 7-by-11-inch (18-by-28-cm) oval baking dish works well. Spoon the broth-cream mixture over the vegetables. Cover tightly with aluminum foil and bake for 20 minutes.

❀ Season the chicken breast with salt and pepper. Carefully uncover the baking dish, place the chicken on the bed of vegetables, cover, and bake for 15 minutes. Uncover and bake until the chicken is cooked through, about 5 minutes longer.

❀ Transfer the chicken to a warmed shallow serving bowl and spoon the contents of the baking dish over and around the breast.

NUTRITIONAL ANALYSIS PER SERVING: Calories 292 (Kilojoules 1,226); Protein 28 g; Carbohydrates 14 g; Total Fat 13 g; Saturated Fat 7 g; Cholesterol 107 mg; Sodium 360 mg; Dietary Fiber 2 g

Baked Sea Bass with Olive Vinaigrette

PREP TIME: 20 MINUTES

COOKING TIME: 20 MINUTES

INGREDIENTS

FOR THE OLIVE VINAIGRETTE

1 red bell pepper (capsicum)

4 black olives, pitted and chopped

4 green olives, pitted and chopped

1 small clove garlic, minced

2 teaspoons minced fresh parsley

1 teaspoon capers, chopped

1 tablespoon extra-virgin olive oil

1 teaspoon lemon juice

salt and ground pepper to taste

1 teaspoon olive oil

1 skinless sea bass fillet, about 6 oz (185 g)

salt and ground pepper to taste

1 tablespoon dry white wine

COOKING TIP: Black Niçoise and green picholine olives work well together here. You can find them in the deli sections of well-stocked food stores. If unavailable, substitute any other good-quality black and green cured olives.

A well-seasoned vinaigrette enhanced with olives, capers, and herbs makes a quick sauce for baked fish. You will have roasted bell pepper left over; if desired, slice it and add to a butter (Boston) lettuce or escarole (Batavian endive) salad, or reserve it for a sandwich the following day.

❊ To make the vinaigrette, preheat a broiler (griller). Cut the bell pepper in half lengthwise and remove the stem, seeds, and ribs. Place, cut sides down, on a baking sheet. Broil (grill) until the skins blacken and blister. Remove from the broiler, drape the bell pepper loosely with aluminum foil, and let cool for 10 minutes, then peel away the skin. Finely dice one-fourth of the bell pepper. Reserve the remaining three-fourths of the pepper for another use.

❊ In a small bowl, whisk together the diced bell pepper, black and green olives, garlic, parsley, capers, extra-virgin olive oil, and lemon juice. Season with salt and pepper. Set aside.

❊ Preheat an oven to 375°F (190°C).

❊ Put the 1 teaspoon olive oil in a small baking dish. Add the sea bass and turn to coat. Season with salt and pepper. Spoon the wine around the fish. Bake until the fish is opaque throughout and just flakes with a fork, 12–15 minutes.

❊ Using a spatula, transfer the fish to a warmed dinner plate. Top with the olive vinaigrette.

NUTRITIONAL ANALYSIS PER SERVING: Calories 389 (Kilojoules 1,634); Protein 32 g; Carbohydrates 6 g; Total Fat 26 g; Saturated Fat 4 g; Cholesterol 70 mg; Sodium 753 mg; Dietary Fiber 2 g

Italian Sausage with Peperonata

PREP TIME: 15 MINUTES

COOKING TIME: 50 MINUTES

INGREDIENTS

1½ tablespoons olive oil

¼ yellow onion or 1 small leek, white and pale green parts only, thinly sliced

1 clove garlic, minced

⅓ cup (2 oz/60 g) grated plum (Roma) tomato *(see glossary, page 111)*

1 red bell pepper (capsicum), seeded and thinly sliced lengthwise

6 fresh basil leaves, torn into small pieces

salt and ground pepper to taste

1 tablespoon water

1 Italian pork, turkey, or chicken sausage, 4–6 oz (125–185 g)

COOKING TIP: For a vegetarian version, make the peperonata without the sausage, and spoon it over polenta or pasta.

For an authentic Italian taste, look for a sausage seasoned with fennel seeds. If you can't find one, add a pinch of fennel seeds to the tomato-and-pepper mixture. Spoon over polenta and serve with some crusty bread on the side.

✹ In a small frying pan over medium-low heat, warm 1 tablespoon of the olive oil. Add the onion or leek and the garlic and sauté until softened, about 5 minutes. Add the tomato and sauté until flavor develops, about 5 minutes. Add the bell pepper, basil, salt, and pepper and stir well. Add the water, cover, and simmer gently until the pepper is tender, 25–30 minutes, adding a little more water if the mixture looks too dry. Transfer to a bowl.

✹ Rinse the frying pan and return to medium heat. Add the remaining ½ tablespoon olive oil to the frying pan. Prick the sausage in 3 or 4 places with a knife, add to the frying pan, and cook until it is brown on all sides and no longer pink inside, about 10 minutes. Pierce with a knife to check doneness. Transfer to a cutting board. Pour off any fat in the frying pan, add the pepper mixture, and reheat gently.

✹ Cut the sausage on the diagonal into slices ½ inch (12 mm) thick. Transfer the pepper mixture to a dinner plate and top with the sausage.

NUTRITIONAL ANALYSIS PER SERVING: Calories 588 (Kilojoules 2,470); Protein 23 g; Carbohydrates 19 g; Total Fat 47 g; Saturated Fat 12 g; Cholesterol 81 mg; Sodium 965 mg; Dietary Fiber 4 g

Baked Swordfish with Tomato-Caper Sauce

PREP TIME: 20 MINUTES

COOKING TIME: 20 MINUTES

INGREDIENTS

1 swordfish steak, 6 oz (185 g)
  and no more than ½ inch
  (12 mm) thick

salt and ground pepper to taste

1 teaspoon plus 1 tablespoon olive oil

1 small clove garlic, minced

pinch of red pepper flakes

½ cup (3 oz/90 g) grated plum (Roma)
  tomato (see glossary, page 111)

½ teaspoon chopped fresh oregano

1 teaspoon chopped capers

1 tablespoon dry white wine

Vary this dish by adding a few chopped olives or anchovies to the sauce, or by replacing the swordfish with tuna or halibut. On another occasion, try the sauce on spaghetti. Doubling the sauce will make enough for ¼ pound (125 g) pasta.

❀ Preheat an oven to 400°F (200°C).

❀ Season the swordfish with salt and pepper. Put the 1 teaspoon olive oil in a small baking dish. Add the swordfish and turn to coat with the oil. Set aside.

❀ In a small frying pan over medium heat, warm the 1 tablespoon olive oil. Add the garlic and sauté for 1 minute to release its fragrance. Add the red pepper flakes, tomato, and oregano and simmer until the mixture is thick and saucelike, about 5 minutes. Stir in the capers. Season to taste with salt. Remove from the heat.

❀ Spoon the white wine around the fish, then bake until the fish is opaque throughout and just flakes with a fork, 10–12 minutes.

❀ Using a spatula, transfer the fish to a warmed dinner plate. Reheat the sauce gently, adding a few drops of water if needed to thin it a bit, then spoon over the fish.

NUTRITIONAL ANALYSIS PER SERVING: Calories 375 (Kilojoules 1,575); Protein 31 g; Carbohydrates 5 g; Total Fat 24 g; Saturated Fat 4 g; Cholesterol 59 mg; Sodium 272 mg; Dietary Fiber 1 g

Hamburger on Garlic Toast with Watercress and Stilton

PREP TIME: 15 MINUTES

COOKING TIME: 10 MINUTES

INGREDIENTS

⅓ lb (155 g) ground (minced) beef chuck

scant ½ teaspoon salt

ground pepper to taste

1 tablespoon finely minced green (spring) onion, white and pale green parts only

1½ teaspoons olive oil

1 oz (30 g) Stilton cheese, at room temperature

1 slice coarse country bread, about ⅓ inch (9 mm) thick

1 clove garlic, halved

½ cup (½ oz/15 g) watercress leaves, thick stems removed

Sometimes only a hamburger will do. Here's an open-faced version made with crisp garlic toast and watercress on the bottom and crumbled Stilton on top. Use extra watercress to make a salad, adding some Belgian endive (chicory/witloof) and a mustard vinaigrette, if you like.

❋ Place the beef in a bowl and season with salt and pepper. Stir in the onion, mixing well. Gently shape into a patty ½ inch (12 mm) thick.

❋ In a small frying pan over high heat, warm the olive oil. When the pan is very hot, add the patty and reduce the heat to medium. Cook until the hamburger is crusty on the underside, about 2 minutes, then turn and cook on the second side until done to your liking, 1–1½ minutes longer for medium-rare. While the hamburger cooks on the second side, crumble half of the Stilton on top. Using a knife, smash the Stilton on top so that it melts onto the hamburger. Transfer the hamburger to a plate; keep warm.

❋ Add the bread slice to the frying pan and cook, turning once, until lightly browned and toasty, 1–2 minutes on each side. Remove from the frying pan and rub one side well with the cut sides of the halved garlic clove. Put the toast on a dinner plate, garlic-rubbed side up. Top with the remaining Stilton, crumbling it evenly over the toast, then with the watercress. Top the watercress with the hamburger and any juices.

NUTRITIONAL ANALYSIS PER SERVING: Calories 578 (Kilojoules 2,428); Protein 36 g; Carbohydrates 23 g; Total Fat 37 g; Saturated Fat 15 g; Cholesterol 112 mg; Sodium 1,872 mg; Dietary Fiber 1 g

Steamed Clams with White Wine, Garlic, and Parsley

PREP TIME: 15 MINUTES

COOKING TIME: 10 MINUTES

INGREDIENTS

¾ cup (6 fl oz/180 ml) dry white wine

1 clove garlic, minced

1 large shallot, minced

½ bay leaf

2 tablespoons minced fresh parsley

1½ lb (750 g) littleneck clams
  (about 18), well scrubbed

1½ tablespoons unsalted butter,
  cut into small pieces

COOKING TIP: For a more substantial main course, toss the cooked clams and their juices with spaghetti or linguine.

Sit down to a steaming bowl of garlicky clams made in less than 30 minutes. You can substitute mussels for the clams, although they will cook a minute or two faster.

❋ In a saucepan over medium-high heat, combine the wine, garlic, shallot, bay leaf, and 1 tablespoon of the parsley. Bring to a simmer and cook for 1 minute. Discard any clams that do not close to the touch, then add the clams to the pan, cover, and steam until they open, 4–5 minutes, shaking the pan once or twice as they cook.

❋ Uncover and discard any clams that haven't opened. Add the butter and stir and toss lightly. Using a slotted spoon, transfer the clams to a large bowl, discarding the bay leaf. Pour the pan juices over them and top with the remaining 1 tablespoon parsley.

NUTRITIONAL ANALYSIS PER SERVING: Calories 384 (Kilojoules 1,613); Protein 15 g; Carbohydrates 12 g; Total Fat 18 g; Saturated Fat 11 g; Cholesterol 82 mg; Sodium 77 mg; Dietary Fiber 1 g

Steak au Poivre with Oven Fries

PREP TIME: 10 MINUTES, PLUS
1 HOUR FOR MARINATING

COOKING TIME: 25 MINUTES

INGREDIENTS

1½ teaspoons mixed peppercorns
   (see note)

1 New York steak, about ¾ lb (375 g)

4 teaspoons olive oil

1 russet potato, about ½ lb (250 g)

salt to taste

COOKING TIP: Letting the steak rest
after cooking allows the juices to
settle, so more of them will stay in
the meat when it's sliced.

You can find jars of mixed peppercorns (usually black, white, pink, and green) in many supermarket spice racks. Or make your own blend of black, white, and green peppercorns.

❈ In a mortar or in a spice grinder, grind the peppercorns until coarsely crushed. Brush the steak on both sides with 2 teaspoons of the olive oil, then press the peppercorns into both sides of the steak, coating evenly. Let stand at room temperature for 1 hour.

❈ Preheat an oven to 450°F (230°C).

❈ Prepare the potato: Cut in half lengthwise, then cut each half into thirds lengthwise to make 6 large fries. Put the potatoes in a bowl with cold water to cover and swish to remove the surface starch. Drain and refill the bowl with cold water. Let the potatoes stand in the water for 5 minutes longer, then swish again, drain well, and pat dry in a clean kitchen towel.

❈ Put a heavy-duty baking sheet in the oven to preheat for 5 minutes. Meanwhile, coat the potato fries with the remaining 2 teaspoons olive oil and sprinkle with salt. When the baking sheet is hot, arrange the potatoes on it, one cut side down. Bake until the bottom sides are browned, 10–15 minutes. Turn to the other cut sides and continue baking until the other sides are browned and the potatoes are tender when pierced, 5–10 minutes longer.

❈ While the potatoes are baking, place a frying pan over medium heat. Season the steak with salt. When the frying pan is hot, add the steak and cook, turning once, until done to your liking, 2–3 minutes on each side for medium-rare. Transfer to a cutting board and let stand for 10 minutes.

❈ Slice the steak on the diagonal. Transfer the slices to a warmed dinner plate, spoon any accumulated juices over them, and arrange the potatoes alongside.

NUTRITIONAL ANALYSIS PER SERVING: Calories 1,016 (Kilojoules 4,267); Protein 64 g; Carbohydrates 43 g; Total Fat 64 g; Saturated Fat 21 g; Cholesterol 183 mg; Sodium 165 mg; Dietary Fiber 5 g

Braised Pork Chop with Caraway Cabbage

PREP TIME: 10 MINUTES

COOKING TIME: 30 MINUTES

INGREDIENTS

1 teaspoon olive oil

1 pork loin chop, about ½ lb (250 g)

salt, ground pepper, and paprika to taste

1 tablespoon unsalted butter

½ small yellow onion, thinly sliced

¼ small head green cabbage, thinly sliced

⅛ teaspoon caraway seeds

STORAGE TIP: Leftover raw cabbage will keep for at least a week in the refrigerator. Shred it for coleslaw or steam wedges and dress them with butter, salt, and paprika.

A bed of shredded cabbage and onion develops a delectable flavor when a pork chop is cooked on top of it. Serve with a favorite mustard, some rye or pumpernickel bread, and a cold beer.

❋ In a frying pan over medium heat, warm the olive oil. Season the pork chop on both sides with salt, pepper, and paprika. When the oil is hot, add the pork chop and brown, turning once, about 1 minute on each side. Transfer to a plate.

❋ Pour off any oil in the frying pan, let the pan cool for about 1 minute, and then add the butter. Return the frying pan to medium-low heat. When the butter melts, add the onion. Sauté until softened, about 5 minutes; do not allow the onion to brown. Add the cabbage and caraway seeds, season with salt and pepper, and stir to mix with the onion. Cover and cook until the cabbage is almost tender, about 10 minutes, lowering the heat if necessary so the vegetables cook without browning.

❋ Put the pork chop on top of the cabbage, cover, and cook over medium-low heat until the pork chop is no longer pink when cut into at the center but is still juicy, about 10 minutes. Do not overcook or it will be dry.

❋ Transfer the cabbage and pork to a warmed dinner plate.

NUTRITIONAL ANALYSIS PER SERVING: Calories 518 (Kilojoules 2,176); Protein 37 g; Carbohydrates 11 g; Total Fat 36 g; Saturated Fat 15 g; Cholesterol 140 mg; Sodium 118 mg; Dietary Fiber 4 g

Orecchiette with Broccoli and Pine Nuts

PREP TIME: 10 MINUTES

COOKING TIME: 25 MINUTES

INGREDIENTS

1 tablespoon pine nuts

½ teaspoon plus 2 tablespoons extra-virgin olive oil

½ lb (250 g) broccoli

¼ lb (125 g) dried orecchiette

1 clove garlic, minced

pinch of red pepper flakes

salt to taste

COOKING TIP: If you can't find orecchiette (ear-shaped pasta), use shells or farfalle instead.

This recipe uses both the broccoli florets and the stems. For best results, choose broccoli with thin stems, which will be more tender. To make a more substantial dish, add 2 ounces (60 g) bulk pork sausage, browning it along with the garlic.

❀ In a small frying pan over medium-low heat, combine the pine nuts and the ½ teaspoon olive oil. Cook, stirring constantly, until the nuts are an even golden brown, about 5 minutes. Pour onto a small plate and set aside.

❀ Separate the broccoli florets from the stems. Using a small knife, peel the stems thickly to reveal the pale green heart. Bring a large saucepan three-fourths full of salted water to a boil over high heat. Add the broccoli florets and stems and cook until both are just tender when pierced with a knife. The florets will cook in about 3 minutes, while the stems may take 5–6 minutes. Using tongs, lift out the broccoli pieces and drain in a sieve. Chop coarsely.

❀ Add the pasta to the same boiling water and cook until al dente (tender but firm to the bite), about 11 minutes or according to package directions.

❀ While the pasta cooks, heat the remaining 2 tablespoons olive oil in a frying pan over medium heat. Add the garlic and red pepper flakes and sauté for 1 minute to release their fragrance. Add the broccoli and pine nuts, season generously with salt, and stir to coat with the seasonings. Cook until the broccoli is heated through.

❀ Drain the pasta, reserving about ¼ cup (2 fl oz/60 ml) of the cooking water. Return the pasta to the warm saucepan. Add the broccoli mixture and toss, adding a tablespoon or two of the cooking water if needed to moisten the pasta. Serve in a warmed bowl.

NUTRITIONAL ANALYSIS PER SERVING: Calories 772 (Kilojoules 3,242); Protein 21 g; Carbohydrates 94 g; Total Fat 37 g; Saturated Fat 5 g; Cholesterol 0 mg; Sodium 47 mg; Dietary Fiber 8 g

Fettuccine with Cherry Tomatoes, Arugula, and Bread Crumbs

PREP TIME: 15 MINUTES

COOKING TIME: 15 MINUTES

INGREDIENTS

¼ cup (½ oz/15 g) fine fresh bread
   crumbs

1 teaspoon plus 1 tablespoon olive oil

1 large clove garlic, minced

⅓ lb (5 oz) cherry tomatoes
   (about 16), stems removed, halved

salt and ground pepper to taste

2 oz (60 g) arugula (rocket), coarsely
   chopped

¼ lb (125 g) fresh fettuccine

COOKING TIP: If you can't find
arugula, substitute 12 fresh basil
leaves. Add them to the sauce when
you add the pasta.

Everybody needs a repertoire of 10-minute pasta sauces such as this one. Make it in summer when cherry tomatoes are at their best. Adding some gold ones would make the dish even prettier.

❀ Preheat an oven to 325°F (165°C). Put the bread crumbs in a pie pan or on a rimmed baking sheet and bake until golden brown, about 10 minutes. Transfer to a bowl and toss with the 1 teaspoon olive oil until evenly coated. Set aside.

❀ Bring a large pot three-fourths full of salted water to a boil over high heat.

❀ Meanwhile, in a frying pan over medium heat, combine the 1 table-spoon olive oil, the garlic, and the cherry tomatoes. Cook gently until the tomatoes release some of their juice, about 2 minutes. Do not allow the tomatoes to collapse completely. Season with salt and pepper and stir in the arugula. Cook just until the arugula wilts slightly—it will wilt more in the heat of the pasta—then reduce the heat to low and keep warm.

❀ Add the pasta to the boiling water and cook until al dente (tender but firm to the bite), 1–2 minutes. Drain and transfer to the frying pan. Toss to coat well with the sauce.

❀ Transfer to a warmed bowl. Top with the toasted crumbs.

NUTRITIONAL ANALYSIS PER SERVING: Calories 574 (Kilojoules 2,411); Protein 17 g; Carbohydrates 79 g; Total Fat 22 g; Saturated Fat 3 g; Cholesterol 83 mg; Sodium 128 mg; Dietary Fiber 5 g

Portobello Mushroom "Steak" with Garlic Butter

PREP TIME: 10 MINUTES

COOKING TIME: 25 MINUTES

INGREDIENTS

1½ tablespoons olive oil

1 fresh portobello mushroom, about ½ lb (250 g) and 4½ inches (11.5 cm) in diameter, brushed clean and stem removed

salt and ground pepper to taste

2 teaspoons unsalted butter

1 large clove garlic, minced

1 teaspoon minced fresh parsley

COOKING TIP: Try making a portobello mushroom burger: Sauté the mushroom as directed but place it, whole, in a toasted hamburger bun. Top with garlic butter and add sliced onion, lettuce, tomato, or other condiments of your choice.

The common cultivated brown mushroom, also called cremini, becomes the full-flavored, dark-gilled portobello when allowed to grow for a few more days. Slowly browned in a frying pan, then sliced and topped with garlic butter, a meaty portobello can be as satisfying as a steak.

❀ In a small frying pan over medium-high heat, warm the olive oil. Add the mushroom, rounded side down. Season the gill side liberally with salt and pepper and reduce the heat to medium-low. Cook for 5 minutes, then turn, season with salt and pepper, and cook, turning every 5 minutes, until tender and well browned on the rounded side, about 15 minutes longer. Transfer to a cutting board.

❀ Remove the frying pan from the heat. Let cool for a minute or two, then add the butter, garlic, and parsley. Swirl the pan to melt the butter and to cook the garlic briefly; if the pan has cooled too much, return it to low heat until the butter melts.

❀ Cut the mushroom into slices. Add any mushroom juices to the frying pan. Transfer the mushroom slices to a warmed dinner plate. Pour the garlic butter over them.

NUTRITIONAL ANALYSIS PER SERVING: Calories 304 (Kilojoules 1,277); Protein 5 g; Carbohydrates 11 g; Total Fat 29 g; Saturated Fat 8 g; Cholesterol 21 mg; Sodium 10 mg; Dietary Fiber 3 g

Fried Rice with Snow Peas, Eggs, and Ham

PREP TIME: 15 MINUTES

COOKING TIME: 10 MINUTES

INGREDIENTS

5 teaspoons peanut oil

1 egg, lightly beaten

¾ cup (2½ oz/75 g) thinly sliced leek, white and pale green parts only

¼ lb (125 g) snow peas (mangetouts), trimmed and cut on the diagonal into ½-inch (12-mm) pieces

2 cups (10 oz/315 g) cold, cooked white rice

2 oz (60 g) cooked ham, diced

salt and ground pepper to taste

1 teaspoon Asian sesame oil

Generations of Chinese cooks have perfected the method for turning leftover rice into an economical feast. By adding snow peas, leeks, ham, and egg—or, on another occasion, English peas, mushrooms, sliced cooked sausage, or cooked chicken—you can transform unpromising day-old rice into a memorable one-dish meal.

❀ In a nonstick frying pan over medium-high heat, warm 1 teaspoon of the peanut oil. When the oil is hot, add the egg and swirl to make a thin pancake. As it sets, lift the edges of the pancake, tilting the pan to allow any uncooked egg to run underneath. When the pancake is set but still moist, transfer to a bowl. Allow it to set for a minute or so, then chop coarsely.

❀ Wipe out the frying pan with a paper towel and return to medium-high heat. When the pan is hot, add the remaining 4 teaspoons peanut oil. When the oil is hot, add the leek and snow peas. Add a few drops of water to create steam, then toss and stir until the vegetables are slightly softened, 2–3 minutes. Add the rice and toss and stir until hot throughout, about 3 minutes, separating the grains with a spatula or wooden spoon. Add the ham and reserved egg and toss and stir for about 30 seconds longer. Season with salt and pepper.

❀ Drizzle the sesame oil over the fried rice and toss a few times to blend, then transfer to a warmed bowl.

NUTRITIONAL ANALYSIS PER SERVING: Calories 872 (Kilojoules 3,662); Protein 31 g; Carbohydrates 99 g; Total Fat 38 g; Saturated Fat 8 g; Cholesterol 246 mg; Sodium 935 mg; Dietary Fiber 5 g

Eggplant Parmesan

PREP TIME: 20 MINUTES

COOKING TIME: 35 MINUTES

INGREDIENTS

2 Asian (slender) eggplants
(aubergines), 6–8 oz (185–250 g)
total weight

1 tablespoon plus 2 teaspoons
olive oil

salt and ground pepper to taste

1 clove garlic, minced

⅔ cup (4 oz/125 g) grated plum
(Roma) tomato (see glossary,
page 111)

4 fresh basil leaves, torn into small
pieces

⅔ cup (2½ oz/75 g) shredded
whole-milk mozzarella cheese

2 tablespoons grated Parmesan
cheese

MAKE-AHEAD TIP: You can assemble
the dish several hours ahead and
bake when you are ready for dinner.

Although many people think of eggplant Parmesan as a dish that yields many servings, it's easy to make a serving for one. Use Asian eggplants and you'll have no waste or leftovers.

❊ Preheat a broiler (griller).

❊ Trim the ends off the eggplants, then cut lengthwise into slices ¼ inch (6 mm) thick. Using the 1 tablespoon olive oil, lightly brush both sides of the eggplant slices and arrange on a baking sheet. Season with salt and pepper. Slip under the broiler and broil (grill) until lightly browned, 4–5 minutes. Turn and broil until lightly browned on the second side, about 4 minutes longer. Transfer the slices to paper towels to drain.

❊ Preheat an oven to 375°F (190°C).

❊ In a small frying pan over medium heat, warm the 2 teaspoons olive oil. Add the garlic and sauté for 1 minute to release its fragrance. Add the tomato and basil and season with salt and pepper. Simmer briskly, stirring often, until the mixture forms a sauce, about 5 minutes. Remove from the heat.

❊ Choose a baking dish just large enough to hold the eggplant in 2 layers. Arrange half of the eggplant in the baking dish, then spread with half of the tomato sauce. Top with half of the mozzarella. Repeat the layers, then top with the Parmesan cheese.

❊ Bake until bubbling hot and the cheese is nicely browned, about 20 minutes. Let cool for 10 minutes before eating.

NUTRITIONAL ANALYSIS PER SERVING: Calories 525 (Kilojoules 2,205); Protein 21 g; Carbohydrates 21 g; Total Fat 41 g; Saturated Fat 14 g; Cholesterol 63 mg; Sodium 469 mg; Dietary Fiber 5 g

Spring Vegetable Stew with Couscous

PREP TIME: 25 MINUTES

COOKING TIME: 20 MINUTES

INGREDIENTS

juice of ½ lemon

1 large artichoke

1 tablespoon olive oil

1 leek, white and pale green parts only, halved lengthwise and thinly sliced

salt and ground pepper to taste

1 medium or 2 small turnips, peeled and cut into bite-sized pieces

¾ cup (4 oz/125 g) shelled English peas

1 tablespoon cold water, if needed

3 teaspoons unsalted butter

½ cup (3 oz/90 g) instant couscous

½ cup (4 fl oz/125 ml) boiling water

1 tablespoon chopped fresh mint

grated zest of ½ lemon

COOKING TIP: Steam the artichoke leaves the next day and enjoy them with mayonnaise or lemon butter.

Feel free to adapt this vegetable stew according to what you find in the market. Asparagus tips, baby carrots, and fava (broad) beans would make suitable additions or substitutions.

❁ Fill a small bowl three-fourths full with water and add the lemon juice. To trim the artichoke, pull back the tough outer leaves until they break at the base; discard or reserve for another use. Keep removing the leaves until you reach the tender, yellow-green heart. Using a serrated knife, cut across the artichoke to remove the top 1–1½ inches (2.5–4 cm). Cut off the stem at the base. Using a small knife, trim the base so no dark green parts remain. Cut the artichoke in half lengthwise. Using a spoon, scrape out the hairy "choke" and prickly tipped inner leaves. Cut each half lengthwise into 4 equal wedges and place in the lemon water to prevent oxidizing.

❁ In a nonaluminum frying pan over medium heat, warm the olive oil. Add the leek and sauté until softened, about 3 minutes. Drain the artichoke wedges and add to the frying pan. Season with salt and pepper and stir to coat with the oil. Cover, reduce the heat to medium-low, and cook until the artichoke wedges are almost tender, about 10 minutes. Add the turnips and peas and season again with salt and pepper. If the mixture looks dry, add the cold water. Bring to a simmer, cover, and cook until the peas and turnips are tender, about 5 minutes. If necessary, add just enough additional water to keep the mixture from drying out.

❁ While the vegetables cook, in a small saucepan over medium heat, melt 2 teaspoons of the butter. Add the couscous and stir constantly until lightly toasted, 3–4 minutes. Add the boiling water, cover, and remove from the heat. Let stand for 8 minutes, then uncover, add the remaining 1 teaspoon butter, and fluff with a fork until the grains are separate. Season with salt.

❁ Combine the couscous, vegetables, mint, and lemon zest and toss lightly with a fork. Taste and adjust the seasonings. Transfer to a warmed dinner plate.

NUTRITIONAL ANALYSIS PER SERVING: Calories 789 (Kilojoules 3,314); Protein 25 g; Carbohydrates 118 g; Total Fat 27 g; Saturated Fat 9 g; Cholesterol 31 mg; Sodium 259 mg; Dietary Fiber 19 g

Spicy Macaroni and Cheese

PREP TIME: 20 MINUTES IF USING FRESH CHILE; 10 MINUTES IF USING CANNED

COOKING TIME: 40 MINUTES

INGREDIENTS

1 small fresh poblano chile or 2 tablespoons canned chopped green chile

3 teaspoons unsalted butter

2 tablespoons fine cracker (savory biscuit) crumbs

2 teaspoons all-purpose (plain) flour

½ cup (4 fl oz/125 ml) milk, plus more as needed for thinning

¼ teaspoon salt

pinch of red pepper flakes

generous 1 cup (3 oz/90 g) fusilli (corkscrews)

1 cup (4 oz/125 g) finely shredded cheddar cheese

PREP TIP: To make fine crumbs without a food processor, put the crackers between two sheets of waxed paper and crush with a rolling pin.

Adding fresh green chile gives this old-fashioned favorite new life. Serve with a salad of lettuce, tomato, and red (Spanish) onion and a cold beer.

⊛ Preheat an oven to 350°F (180°C).

⊛ If using a fresh chile, preheat a broiler (griller). Place the chile on a baking sheet and slip under the broiler. Broil (grill), turning as needed, until the skin blackens and blisters. Remove from the broiler, drape loosely with aluminum foil, and let cool slightly, then peel away the skin and remove the stem and seeds. Dice the chile neatly. You will need 2 tablespoons; reserve any extra for soup, salad, or a grilled cheese sandwich.

⊛ Bring a large saucepan three-fourths full of salted water to a boil over high heat.

⊛ Meanwhile, in a small saucepan over medium-low heat, melt the butter. Put the cracker crumbs in a small bowl, add 1 teaspoon of the melted butter, and stir to coat.

⊛ Add the flour to the butter remaining in the saucepan and cook, whisking, until well blended, about 1 minute. Whisk in the ½ cup (4 fl oz/ 125 ml) milk and add the salt, red pepper flakes, and chile. Cook, whisking constantly, until the mixture comes to a simmer and thickens, about 3 minutes. Reduce the heat to low and continue to cook, whisking occasionally, while you prepare the pasta. The sauce should be pourable; if it gets too thick, add a little milk.

⊛ Add the pasta to the boiling water and cook for 5 minutes; it will be underdone. Drain and return the pasta to the pan. Add the sauce and all but 2 tablespoons of the cheddar cheese. Stir until the cheese melts. Transfer to a small baking dish; an oval 8-by-5-inch (20-by-13-cm) ramekin works well. Top with the remaining cheese and then with the cracker crumbs.

⊛ Bake until bubbling hot, 15–20 minutes. Let cool for a few minutes before eating.

NUTRITIONAL ANALYSIS PER SERVING: Calories 1,145 (Kilojoules 4,809); Protein 47 g; Carbohydrates 101 g; Total Fat 62 g; Saturated Fat 35 g; Cholesterol 167 mg; Sodium 1,545 mg; Dietary Fiber 5 g

Linguine with Mussels and Spicy Tomato Sauce

PREP TIME: 15 MINUTES

COOKING TIME: 15 MINUTES

INGREDIENTS

¼ lb (125 g) dried linguine or spaghetti

1 tablespoon olive oil

1 clove garlic, minced

⅛ teaspoon red pepper flakes

½ cup (3 oz/90 g) grated plum (Roma) tomato (see glossary, page 111) or finely chopped canned tomato

2 teaspoons minced fresh parsley

12 mussels, well scrubbed and debearded

PREP TIP: Be sure to buy tightly closed mussels. If some are starting to open, hold them under cold running water and press them closed; if they fail to stay closed, discard them. Wash mussels well and pull out the hairy "beard" if it is still attached. Farm-raised mussels are generally cleaner than wild ones.

You can make this zesty sauce in less time than it takes to cook the pasta. Try replacing the mussels with peeled shrimp for another seafood sauce, or use a combination of mussels, clams, and shrimp.

❊ Bring a large pot three-fourths full of salted water to a boil over high heat. Add the pasta and cook until almost al dente (tender but firm to the bite), about 10 minutes or according to package directions.

❊ While the pasta cooks, in a large frying pan over medium heat, warm the olive oil. Add the garlic and red pepper flakes and sauté for 1 minute to release their fragrance. Add the tomato and 1 teaspoon of the parsley and sauté, stirring constantly, until the flavors blend, about 5 minutes. Discard any mussels that do not close to the touch, then add the remainder to the frying pan. Cover and cook, shaking the pan once or twice, until the mussels open, about 3 minutes. Discard any that do not open.

❊ When the pasta is just slightly underdone, use long tongs to transfer it, dripping wet, to the frying pan. Toss with the sauce and simmer for 1–2 minutes to allow the pasta to finish cooking and absorb the sauce.

❊ Transfer to a warmed bowl. Top with the remaining 1 teaspoon parsley.

NUTRITIONAL ANALYSIS PER SERVING: Calories 647 (Kilojoules 2,717); Protein 27 g; Carbohydrates 94 g; Total Fat 18 g; Saturated Fat 3 g; Cholesterol 27 mg; Sodium 292 mg; Dietary Fiber 4 g

Saffron Risotto with Scallops

PREP TIME: 15 MINUTES

COOKING TIME: 25 MINUTES

INGREDIENTS

1 cup (8 fl oz/250 ml) bottled clam juice

1 cup (8 fl oz/250 ml) water

about ⅛ teaspoon saffron threads

¼ lb (125 g) bay scallops or sea scallops

2 teaspoons olive oil

salt and ground pepper to taste

2 green (spring) onions, white and pale green parts only, minced

1 small clove garlic, minced

½ cup (3½ oz/105 g) Arborio rice

2 tablespoons dry white wine

2 teaspoons unsalted butter

1 teaspoon minced fresh parsley

Treat yourself to a creamy seafood risotto with the heady fragrance of saffron. This recipe makes a generous main course that needs only a salad before or after.

❋ In a small saucepan over medium heat, combine the clam juice, water, and saffron. Bring just to a simmer, taste, and add more saffron if the saffron flavor is not strong enough. Be careful, however: too much saffron can impart a medicinal taste. Keep the mixture hot but not simmering.

❋ If using sea scallops, cut into ½-inch (12-mm) pieces. In a small saucepan wide enough to hold the scallops in a single layer, heat 1 teaspoon of the olive oil over high heat. When the oil is very hot, add the scallops, season with salt and pepper, and sauté just until lightly browned, less than 1 minute. Transfer to a plate.

❋ Reduce the heat to medium and return the saucepan to the heat. Add the remaining 1 teaspoon olive oil, the green onions, and the garlic. Sauté until the onions are softened, about 1 minute. Add the rice and stir until hot throughout, about 1 minute. Add the wine and cook, stirring, until it is absorbed, about 1 minute. Begin adding the hot broth ¼ cup (2 fl oz/60 ml) at a time, stirring often and adding more liquid only when the previous addition has been absorbed. Adjust the heat so that the rice simmers steadily but not briskly. It should take about 20 minutes for the rice to absorb the liquid and become creamy and al dente (tender but firm to the bite). You may not need all the liquid; if you need more, use hot water.

❋ When the rice is almost done, stir in the reserved scallops, butter, and parsley. Season with salt and pepper. Enjoy immediately.

NUTRITIONAL ANALYSIS PER SERVING: Calories 616 (Kilojoules 2,587); Protein 27 g; Carbohydrates 79 g; Total Fat 19 g; Saturated Fat 6 g; Cholesterol 58 mg; Sodium 707 mg; Dietary Fiber 7 g

Chinese Noodles with Chicken and Baby Bok Choy

PREP TIME: 15 MINUTES

COOKING TIME: 20 MINUTES

INGREDIENTS

2 cups (16 fl oz/500 ml) chicken broth

I cup (8 fl oz/250 ml) water

I skinless, boneless chicken breast
half, at room temperature

2 baby bok choy

1½ tablespoons peanut oil

⅛ teaspoon red pepper flakes,
or more to taste

salt to taste

⅓ lb (155 g) fresh Chinese egg
noodles

3 green (spring) onions, white and
pale green parts only, minced

⅓ cup (½ oz/15 g) coarsely chopped
fresh cilantro (fresh coriander)

¼ cup (1½ oz/45 g) coarsely chopped
roasted peanuts

2 teaspoons Thai or Vietnamese fish
sauce

COOKING TIP: Keep extra Chinese
egg noodles in the freezer for quick
meals. Add directly to boiling water,
drain when al dente, and add to a
bowl of chicken broth with sliced
green onion, chopped cilantro, and
a drizzle of sesame oil.

Fresh Chinese egg noodles (also known as chow mein noodles), available in Chinese markets and the refrigerated section of some food stores, offer a good alternative to fresh Italian pasta. To complete this quickly made meal-in-a-bowl, you need only add a cold beer or some chilled white wine.

❀ In a small saucepan over high heat, combine the broth and water. Bring to a simmer over high heat. Add the chicken, cover, and remove from the heat. Let stand until the chicken is cooked throughout, about 15 minutes. Remove the chicken, reserving the broth for another use. When cool enough to handle, shred the chicken by hand.

❀ Separate the individual leaves of bok choy from the central core. Cut all but the smallest leaves in half lengthwise. Discard the core.

❀ Bring a large saucepan three-fourths full of salted water to a boil over high heat.

❀ Meanwhile, in a frying pan over medium heat, warm the peanut oil. Add the red pepper flakes and cook for a few seconds to release their fragrance, then add the bok choy. Season with salt and stir to coat with the oil. Cover and cook until just tender, about 3 minutes.

❀ While the bok choy cooks, add the noodles to the boiling water. Cook until al dente (tender but firm to the bite), 3 minutes or more depending on thickness and freshness.

❀ Drain the noodles and add to the frying pan along with the chicken, green onions, cilantro, peanuts, and fish sauce. Toss briefly to heat through and mix well, then transfer to a warmed bowl.

NUTRITIONAL ANALYSIS PER SERVING: Calories 1,102 (Kilojoules 4,628); Protein 62 g; Carbohydrates 101 g; Total Fat 52 g; Saturated Fat 8 g; Cholesterol 175 mg; Sodium 2,598 mg; Dietary Fiber 9 g

Lemon Custard

PREP TIME: 5 MINUTES

COOKING TIME: 40 MINUTES

INGREDIENTS

1 cup (8 fl oz/250 ml) milk

2½ tablespoons sugar

3 lemon zest strips

pinch of salt

2 egg yolks

boiling water, as needed

A soft baked custard always appeals as a soothing end to a meal. This recipe makes enough for two desserts, unless you succumb to eating one as your breakfast the next morning.

MAKES 2 SERVINGS

❋ Preheat an oven to 350°F (180°C).

❋ In a small saucepan over medium heat, combine the milk, sugar, lemon zest, and salt. Cook, stirring to dissolve the sugar, until bubbles appear along the edges of the pan, about 5 minutes. Remove from the heat.

❋ In a bowl, whisk the egg yolks just until blended. Gradually whisk in the hot milk mixture. Pour the mixture through a fine-mesh sieve into a bowl or large measuring pitcher.

❋ Divide between two ¾-cup (6–fl oz/180-ml) custard cups.

❋ Place the cups in a baking dish large enough to hold them without touching. Carefully add boiling water to the baking dish to reach halfway up the sides of the cups. Bake until the custard looks set when you jiggle the cup gently, about 30 minutes. Remove from the water bath, cool, and chill before eating.

NUTRITIONAL ANALYSIS PER SERVING: Calories 195 (Kilojoules 819); Protein 7 g; Carbohydrates 22 g; Total Fat 9 g; Saturated Fat 4 g; Cholesterol 230 mg; Sodium 137 mg; Dietary Fiber 0 g

Individual Apple Crisp

PREP TIME: 15 MINUTES

COOKING TIME: 40 MINUTES,
   PLUS 15 MINUTES FOR
   COOLING

INGREDIENTS

1 apple, preferably Golden Delicious

2 teaspoons granulated sugar

2 tablespoons all-purpose (plain) flour

1½ teaspoons brown sugar

pinch of ground cinnamon

pinch of salt

1 tablespoon unsalted butter, at room
   temperature

1 tablespoon rolled oats

1½ tablespoons chopped walnuts

Enjoy this rustic dessert warm with a dollop of crème fraîche or lightly sweetened whipped cream. You can use the crisp topping on other fruits in season, such as peaches or berries.

❀ Preheat an oven to 375°F (190°C).

❀ Quarter, core, and peel the apple. Cut each quarter crosswise into slices ¼ inch (6 mm) thick and place in a bowl. Add 1 teaspoon of the granulated sugar and toss to coat evenly.

❀ In another bowl, stir together the remaining 1 teaspoon granulated sugar, the flour, brown sugar, cinnamon, and salt. Add the butter and rub in with your fingers until well distributed and coated with flour. Add the oats and work with your fingers until the mixture forms clumps. Stir in the walnuts.

❀ Put the apple slices in a small baking dish; a 7-by-4-inch (18-by-10-cm) oval baking dish works well. Pat into an even layer. Sprinkle the topping evenly over the apple slices.

❀ Bake until the topping is well browned and the apple is tender, about 40 minutes. Remove from the oven and let cool for 15 minutes before eating.

NUTRITIONAL ANALYSIS PER SERVING: Calories 398 (Kilojoules 1,672); Protein 4 g; Carbohydrates 56 g; Total Fat 19 g; Saturated Fat 8 g; Cholesterol 31 mg; Sodium 145 mg; Dietary Fiber 4 g

Warm Broiled Banana with Apricot Jam

PREP TIME: 5 MINUTES

COOKING TIME: 10 MINUTES

INGREDIENTS

1 very ripe banana, unpeeled, ends removed, and halved lengthwise

1 tablespoon apricot jam

2 teaspoons unsalted butter

⅓ cup (3 fl oz/80 ml) vanilla ice cream

COOKING TIP: Be sure to let the banana get fully ripe—the skin should be speckled with black spots—or it will be too starchy to cook properly.

When broiled, a halved ripe banana turns as soft and creamy as custard. Slip the halves from their skins with two forks and put the vanilla ice cream on top.

❋ Position a rack in a broiler (griller) about 7 inches (18 cm) from the heat source and preheat the broiler.

❋ Put the banana halves in a flameproof baking dish, cut sides up. Slip under the broiler and broil (grill) until the banana halves offer no resistance to a fork and begin to brown, about 7 minutes.

❋ While the banana cooks, in a small saucepan over medium heat, combine the jam and butter. Heat, stirring, until the butter melts and the mixture is smooth and creamy.

❋ When the banana has begun to brown, remove from the broiler and spoon the jam mixture over the halves. Return to the broiler and broil until the topping bubbles, 1–2 minutes.

❋ Slip the banana halves from their skins and transfer to a plate, spooning any juices in the baking dish over them. Put the vanilla ice cream on top.

NUTRITIONAL ANALYSIS PER SERVING: Calories 309 (Kilojoules 1,298); Protein 3 g; Carbohydrates 50 g; Total Fat 13 g; Saturated Fat 8 g; Cholesterol 40 mg; Sodium 45 mg; Dietary Fiber 2 g

Sliced Peach with Whipped Ricotta and Honey

PREP TIME: 10 MINUTES

COOKING TIME: 10 MINUTES
     IF USING NUTS

INGREDIENTS

2 teaspoons pistachio nuts (optional)

⅓ cup (3 oz/90 g) whole-milk ricotta
cheese

2 teaspoons honey

1 small ripe peach

Whipped ricotta has the seductive, creamy texture of the more expensive mascarpone cheese. You might want to double this recipe and use the extra cheese on your breakfast toast in place of butter and jam, or with other fresh fruits such as apricots, berries, figs, apples, or pears.

⊛ If using the pistachios, preheat an oven to 325°F (165°C). Spread the nuts in a pie pan and place in the oven until fragrant and beginning to brown, 8–10 minutes. Chop and set aside.

⊛ In a blender or a small food processor, combine the ricotta and honey. Process until completely smooth and creamy.

⊛ Peel the peach, if you like. Pit and slice the peach and arrange the slices on a dessert plate, leaving room for the cheese. Spoon the whipped cheese onto the plate and top, if using, with the toasted nuts.

NUTRITIONAL ANALYSIS PER SERVING: Calories 247 (Kilojoules 1,037); Protein 11 g; Carbohydrates 29 g; Total Fat 11 g; Saturated Fat 7 g; Cholesterol 43 mg; Sodium 72 mg; Dietary Fiber 2 g

Chocolate Pudding

PREP TIME: 10 MINUTES

COOKING TIME: 5 MINUTES

INGREDIENTS

3 tablespoons sugar

1 tablespoon cornstarch (cornflour)

1 tablespoon unsweetened cocoa
powder

pinch of salt

1 cup (8 fl oz/250 ml) milk

1 oz (30 g) semisweet (plain)
chocolate, chopped

2 teaspoons unsalted butter

¼ teaspoon vanilla extract (essence)

Old-fashioned chocolate pudding never fails to delight the child in all of us, especially when it is served with a dollop of softly whipped cream on top. This 15-minute recipe makes two portions, for two meals' worth of pleasure.

MAKES 2 SERVINGS

❊ In a small saucepan, stir together the sugar, cornstarch, cocoa, and salt until well blended and no lumps remain. Gradually add ½ cup (4 fl oz/125 ml) of the milk, whisking until smooth, then whisk in the remaining ½ cup (4 fl oz/125 ml) milk. Add the chopped chocolate.

❊ Place over medium heat and bring to a boil, stirring constantly. Boil for 1 minute; the mixture will thicken considerably. Remove from the heat and stir in the butter and vanilla.

❊ Divide between 2 custard cups. Cover while hot and chill before eating.

NUTRITIONAL ANALYSIS PER SERVING: Calories 272 (Kilojoules 1,142); Protein 5 g; Carbohydrates 39 g; Total Fat 13 g; Saturated Fat 8 g; Cholesterol 27 mg; Sodium 133 mg; Dietary Fiber 2 g

Poached Pear with Ginger Syrup

PREP TIME: 5 MINUTES

COOKING TIME: 30 MINUTES

INGREDIENTS

½ cup (4 fl oz/125 ml) dry white wine

½ cup (4 fl oz/125 ml) water

⅓ cup (3 oz/90 g) sugar

2 peeled fresh ginger slices

1 ripe but firm pear, preferably Bartlett (Williams') or Bosc

½ lemon

COOKING TIP: Pears at the market are almost always underripe. Buy your pear a couple of days ahead and let it ripen at room temperature. It is ready when the stem end gives to gentle pressure.

These delicate pear halves in light syrup would be as appealing on a Sunday morning as after a rich winter supper. Accompany with a few gingersnaps or biscotti.

✻ In a small saucepan, combine the wine, water, and sugar. Smash the ginger slices with the flat side of a large knife blade and add to the pan. Bring to a simmer over medium heat, stirring to dissolve the sugar.

✻ Meanwhile, peel the pear, then halve it and remove the core. Squeeze a little lemon juice on the pear halves to keep them from turning brown, then add them to the simmering liquid, cut sides down. Cover partially and adjust the heat to maintain a gentle simmer. Cook for 15 minutes, then gently turn the pear halves over, cover partially, and cook until a knife just slips in easily, about 5 minutes longer or as needed; the timing depends upon the size and ripeness of the pear. Do not overcook, as it will continue to cook while it cools.

✻ Using a slotted spoon, transfer the pear halves to a lidded container. Raise the heat under the pan to high and simmer the liquid until reduced to ½ cup (4 fl oz/125 ml). Remove from the heat, let cool completely, and remove and discard the ginger slices. Pour the syrup over the pear halves. Cover and chill before eating.

NUTRITIONAL ANALYSIS PER SERVING: Calories 521 (Kilojoules 2,188); Protein 1 g; Carbohydrates 115 g; Total Fat 1 g; Saturated Fat 1 g; Cholesterol 0 mg; Sodium 7 mg; Dietary Fiber 4 g

GLOSSARY

ANCHOVY FILLETS
A slender, tiny relative of the sardine, the anchovy is most commonly preserved by salting its fillets and then packing them in olive oil. The sharp-flavored, briny fillets are used as a salty seasoning.

ARUGULA
This spicy, slightly bitter green, also known as rocket, is native to the Mediterranean, where it is standard salad-bowl fare. The long, multilobed leaves hide grit and must be rinsed well before use.

CHEESES
Their ability to add rich flavor and texture to many dishes make cheeses a versatile staple. Dozens of different types are available in well-stocked food stores and delicatessens and in cheese shops. Those used in this book include:

BLUE-VEINED CHEESE, MILD
Distinguished by veins of blue or blue-green mold, tangy flavor, and texture ranging from creamy to crumbly. Commonly stocked mild varieties include English Stilton and Italian Cambozola.

FETA
Tangy and crumbly, this rich white cheese, traditionally made from sheep's milk, is widely produced in its native Greece and Turkey as well as in Bulgaria, France, and elsewhere.

GOAT CHEESES
Sharply tangy goat cheeses, also known by the generic French term *chèvre,* are made in innumerable varieties. The types most commonly available are fresh and creamy and sold in small rounds or logs.

BEETS
Known by their familiar red color, although golden, pink, white, and even red-and-white-striped varieties are also available, beets are too often cooked until their texture is disappointingly soft and their flavor is diluted. When properly cooked, particularly by roasting, they develop a tender-crisp texture and an irresistible sweetness.

BOK CHOY, BABY
Measuring as little as 4 inches (10 cm) long, this immature form of the popular Chinese cabbage variety is particularly favored for the tender crispness and mild peppery taste of its white-stalked, vibrant green leaves. Young bok choy may be found in well-stocked food stores and farmers' and Asian markets.

MONTEREY JACK
A soft, mild, buttery cow's milk cheese first made in Monterey, California.

MOZZARELLA
A rindless Italian white cheese with a mild taste and soft but dense texture, mozzarella may be found fresh, immersed in water, in well-stocked food stores and Italian delicatessens. Packaged mozzarella is more widely available. Look for whole-milk mozzarella, which has the richest taste and the best melting properties.

PARMESAN
The firm, well-aged cow's milk cheese of Italy is classically used for grating. The finest variety, designated Parmigiano-Reggiano®, is made only from midspring to midautumn, then aged for at least 14 months.

RICOTTA
This light-textured, white, very mild cheese, used in savory and sweet recipes, is produced from whey left over from making other cheeses. Sheep's milk is the traditional base, although cow's milk ricotta is more common.

CAPERS
These unopened flower buds of a bush that grows wild in the Mediterranean are pickled in salt, or a mixture of vinegar and salt, for use whole or chopped as a piquant flavoring or garnish.

CHILES
Many chile varieties exist, in a wide range of shapes, sizes, colors, and heat levels. A chile's heat is concentrated in the interior ribs and in the seeds; discarding them can make a hot chile somewhat milder. You'll find the best chile selection in Latin American, Asian, and farmers' markets. Those called for in this book are the **Anaheim** (below), a slender,

rather flat, generally mild green chile, sometimes referred to as the long green or California chile; the **jalapeño,** the familiar small, fresh green (or less often ripened red) chile with a plump triangular body and thick, slightly sweet, medium-hot to very hot flesh; and the **poblano,** a relatively mild to medium-hot dark green or ripened red chile resembling a tapered, triangular bell pepper.

COUSCOUS, INSTANT
This staple of North Africa is a form of tiny, granular semolina pasta. It cooks to a fluffy consistency for serving as an accompaniment to stews or other saucy dishes. Although from-scratch couscous can take more than an hour to steam, well-stocked food stores sell an "instant" product that has been precooked and redried and is ready in only a few minutes.

EGGPLANT

Also known as aubergine, the eggplant is appreciated for its rich taste and texture. Slender, purple Asian eggplants (below) have a milder flavor and fewer seeds than larger, more rounded globe types. At their peak in summer, eggplants are available year-round.

FENNEL

Looking remarkably like a small, squat, bulbous head of celery, fennel has a crisp texture and a flavor reminiscent of mild, sweet anise. Look for bruise-free pale green bulbs with their feathery leaves intact. Use small amounts of the fragrant leaves in green salads or as a seasoning or garnish.

FISH SAUCE

In Thai and Vietnamese kitchens, where it is known respectively as *nam pla* and *nuoc mam,* this thin, amber-colored liquid made from salted fish is used as a seasoning, much like soy sauce. Fish sauce is sold in most Asian markets and in the Asian foods section of well-stocked food stores. Vietnamese fish sauce tends to be milder than Thai.

GARLIC

Prized for its pungent, highly aromatic flavor, garlic is an indispensable ingredient in many savory dishes. For the best flavor, buy whole heads of dried garlic, separating individual cloves as you need them. Do not buy more than you will use in 1 to 2 weeks.

HERBS

BASIL

Spicy-sweet, tender-leaved basil, an essential seasoning in Mediterranean cooking, goes especially well with poultry, tomatoes, and other vegetables.

BAY LEAVES

The dried whole leaves of the bay laurel tree impart their pungent, spicy flavor to simmered dishes, pickles, and marinades. Seek out the French variety, which has a milder, sweeter flavor than California bay leaves.

CILANTRO

Also known as fresh coriander and Chinese parsley, cilantro has flat, finely notched leaves that resemble those of flat-leaf (Italian) parsley. Its flavor is astringent and slightly grassy.

DILL

This feathery herb has a sprightly, almost sweet taste and delicate aroma best appreciated when the herb is at its freshest, that is, when the leaves and stems are bright green.

MARJORAM

Milder in flavor than its close relative, oregano, this Mediterranean herb complements tomatoes, eggplants (aubergines), poultry, and pork.

MINT

Refreshingly sweet, mint is a popular seasoning for lamb, poultry, vegetables, and fruit. Spearmint is the type most widely sold.

OREGANO

Also known as wild marjoram, this highly aromatic herb, a staple of Italian and Greek cooking, is used fresh or dried in all kinds of savory dishes. It marries particularly well with tomatoes.

PARSLEY

The flat-leaf variety of this herb, also known as Italian parsley, has a more pronounced flavor than the common curly type, making it preferable as a seasoning.

ROSEMARY

Used either fresh or dried, this Mediterranean herb has a strong, aromatic flavor well suited to meats, poultry, seafood, and vegetables.

TARRAGON

With its distinctively sweet flavor reminiscent of anise, tarragon is used fresh to flavor eggs, poultry, vegetables, and salad dressings.

THYME

One of the most important European culinary herbs, thyme delivers a light fragrance and subtle flavor to a wide range of savory foods.

GINGER

Although it resembles a root, this sweet-hot seasoning is actually the underground stem, or rhizome, of the tropical ginger plant.

LEEKS

These members of the Allium family combine a delicate onion flavor with a pleasing edge of sweetness. They can be served hot or cold on their own as a cooked vegetable or can be added to many savory dishes, to which they contribute their distinctive and complex taste. The white root end is often used alone. The tougher green leaves sometimes flavor stocks or other long-cooking dishes.

MUSHROOM, PORTOBELLO

The fully matured form of brown-skinned, ivory-fleshed cremini mushrooms, portobellos are distinguished by their large, flat, circular brown caps and rich taste and texture.

MUSTARD, DIJON

Traditionally made in the French city of Dijon from dark brown mustard seeds (unless otherwise marked *blanc*) and white wine or wine vinegar, Dijon mustard has a distinctive pale color and moderately hot, sharp flavor.

NUTS

Nuts add mellow taste and crunchy texture to sweet and savory dishes alike. For the best selection, look in a specialty-food shop or health-food store. Those used in this book are **pine nuts**, the small, ivory-colored, resinous-tasting nuts extracted from the cones of a species of pine tree; and **pistachios**, rich, slightly sweet nuts with attractively green, crunchy meat. Nuts will keep for several months stored in an airtight container in the freezer.

OLIVES

The fruits of the olive tree are cured in both their unripe green and ripened brownish to black forms, using various combinations of salt, seasonings, brines, vinegars, and oils. Good assortments of cured olives may be found in well-stocked food stores and delicatessens. Among those commonly available are green **picholine** from southeastern France and the small, brownish black **Niçoise** (at right) from Provence.

ONIONS

All kinds of onions lend pungent flavor to savory dishes. **Green onions**, also called spring onions or scallions, are a variety harvested immature, leaves and all, before their bulbs have formed. Both their green tops and white bulbs are appreciated for their mild but still pronounced onion flavor. **Red (Spanish) onions** are a mild, sweet variety with purplish red skin and red-tinged white flesh. **Yellow onions**, the most common type, have white flesh and a strong flavor; they are easily recognized by their dry, yellowish brown skins.

POTATOES

Arguably the most popular of all vegetables, these tubers are sold in many different varieties, distinguished by size, shape, the color and thickness of their skins, and the color and texture of their flesh. **Russet** potatoes, also known as Idahos, are large baking potatoes distinguished by their thick brown skins and a white flesh that cooks to a dry, mealy

OILS

A variety of good-quality oils plays a fundamental role in all kinds of cooking.

OLIVE OIL

No one adjective describes the range of tastes possible in olive oils. Some are spicy with a peppery kick, while others are buttery and mellow. Those labeled "extra-virgin" are generally fruity and full-flavored and are suitable for dressing salads and for use as a condiment. Oils labeled "pure" or simply "olive oil" are blended and more refined, making them best suited to general cooking.

PEANUT OIL

Pale gold and subtly rich, this oil can be heated to fairly high cooking temperatures for frying.

SESAME OIL

Used primarily as a seasoning or condiment, Asian sesame oil burns easily and is rarely used for cooking. Do not confuse this product with lighter, cold-pressed sesame oil sold in health-food stores and well-stocked markets.

VEGETABLE OIL

In recipes, this term applies to seed and vegetable oils—such as canola, safflower, corn—that have bland flavors and may be heated without burning to the high temperatures necessary for frying.

texture. **Red potatoes** (below) are available small to medium-large in size and have white, waxy flesh and red skins.

PROSCIUTTO

The intense flavor and deep pink hue of this Italian cured ham, a specialty of Parma, result from a time-consuming process. The hams, from pigs fed a diet of whey, are cured by dry-salting for one month and then air-drying in cool curing sheds for six months or longer. The unique character of prosciutto is best appreciated when the meat is sliced tissue thin. It can be eaten as an appetizer, on its own or with vegetables or fruits; or it can be chopped to flavor sauces and stuffings.

RADICCHIO

This member of the chicory family is burgundy and white or sometimes green in color, crisp in texture, and has a refreshingly bitter taste. Also known as red chicory, the heads may be round or tapered. The leaves are used raw in salads and appetizers, and the heads, usually halved or quartered, are often grilled or braised.

RICE, ARBORIO

This Italian rice variety has short, round grains that cook to a creamy consistency and chewy texture, making it ideal for the preparation known as risotto. Similar Italian varieties such as Vialone Nano and Carnaroli may be substituted.

SALAD GREENS, MIXED BABY

Many food stores, greengrocers, and farmers' markets carry already mixed assortments of tender baby leaves of lettuce and other salad greens, sold both loose and prepackaged in vacuum-sealed bags. These mixes commonly include butter (Boston) and red leaf lettuces, arugula (rocket), chicory (curly endive), spinach, and radicchio.

SHALLOTS

These coppery-skinned cousins of the onion have a more delicate flavor than their pungent kin. The finely textured flesh is most commonly used as a fragrant seasoning.

TOMATOES

The best tomatoes are found in food stores and farmers' markets at their summertime peak. For especially sweet, juicy flesh, select the round, red or yellow bite-sized variety known as **cherry** tomatoes. For year-round use, use the Italian **plum** variety, also known as the Roma tomato, which is roughly the size and shape of an egg.

When only a small quantity of peeled, seeded, and diced tomato is needed, you can use a box grater rather than the traditional method. Simply cut a plum tomato in half lengthwise and scoop out the seeds with a finger or the handle of a teaspoon. Grate the cut side against the large holes of a handheld grater-shredder, discarding the skin. The resulting tomato pulp blends quickly with other ingredients, cooking to a thick, smooth consistency.

WATERCRESS

Part of the mustard family, these crisp sprigs of round, dark green leaves contribute a refreshingly spicy flavor to salads and make a distinctive garnish for other dishes. Watercress grows wild in freshwater streams in its native Europe and also thrives in commercial cultivation. Its flavor is at its sweetest when picked during the cooler months of spring or autumn.

SPICES

CARAWAY SEEDS

Mildly spicy caraway seeds go especially well with breads and robust-tasting vegetables, poultry, and meats.

CUMIN SEEDS

These potent, crescent-shaped seeds have a strong, dusky aroma and flavor.

FENNEL SEEDS

These small, crescent-shaped seeds come from a plant related to the bulb vegetable of the same name and share with it a mild anise flavor. They complement pork sausage and full-flavored fish.

PAPRIKA

This powdered spice is derived from the dried paprika pepper, available in sweet, mild, and hot forms. Hungarian paprika is considered the best quality, but milder Spanish paprika may also be used.

RED PEPPER FLAKES

The coarsely crushed flesh and whole seeds of dried red chiles, these flakes contribute a touch of moderately hot flavor to sauces and other dishes.

SAFFRON

It takes the hairlike stigmas from many thousands of blossoms of a variety of crocus to yield 1 pound (500 g) of this golden, richly perfumed spice, one of the world's most expensive. Fortunately, just a pinch of saffron will impart a bright, sunny color and heady aroma to a dish. Look for saffron threads; saffron that has been ground loses its flavor more rapidly.

INDEX

ACKNOWLEDGMENTS

The publishers would like to thank the following people and associations for their generous support and assistance in producing this book:
Desne Border, Ken DellaPenta, and Hill Nutrition Associates.

The following kindly lent props for photography: Fillamento, Williams-Sonoma, and Pottery Barn, San Francisco, CA.
The photographer would like to thank Tammy and Mark Becker for generously sharing their home for location photography.
He would also like to thank Chromeworks and ProCamera, San Francisco, CA, and FUJI film for their generous support
of this project. Special acknowledgment goes to Daniel Yearwood for the beautiful backgrounds and surface treatments.